PORTRAITS IN GENESIS:
From Their Point of View

Tony Kessinger

Copyright © 2018 by Tony Kessinger.

ISBN   Paperback   978-1-951469-62-7

All rights reserved. No part of this book may be reproduced or transmitted in any form or by any means, electronic or mechanical, including photocopying, recording, or by any information storage and retrieval system without express written permission from the author, except in the case of brief quotations embodied in critical reviews and certain other non-commercial uses permitted by copyright law.

Printed in the United States of America.

BookWhip
1545 S. Harbor Blvd., #2001,
Fullerton, CA 92832

Disclaimer

The stories in this book are based on factual accounts about eight personalities in the book of Genesis. Whereas the people are real, and the circumstances did occur, the stories go beyond what Scripture has to say. It is the authors attempt to allow the individual personalities to share what conversations, feelings, and emotions may have been part of the biblical narrative.

Each personality speaks from their own perspective in an attempt to encourage the reader to look deeply into the situations presented, adding an element of intrigue to the stories that may or may not have existed. Perhaps the phrase "fact based fiction" could be used to best describe the writing technique utilized in this book.

Dates, places, and ages are accurate. All these factors are taken directly from Scripture so that the reader will be able to understand the importance timing plays in specific events.

Contents

Chapter One	There is a First Time for Everything	1
Chapter Two	His Death Shall Bring Judgment	11
Chapter Three	Judgment	19
Chapter Four	Rest	30
Chapter Five	The Region Beyond	38
Chapter Six	Promises Made	44
Chapter Seven	The Promise Keeper	55
Chapter Eight	Marriage: A Beginning, an Ending, and a Beginning Again	63
Chapter Nine	Isaac and the Challenge of Twin Boys	73
Chapter Ten	Things Are Not Always The Way They Seem	81
Chapter Eleven	Joseph	92

Chapter One

There is a First Time for Everything

Have you ever wondered what it would be like if you were the only person on earth? Well I have experienced that sensation and would like to share with you just how it feels. Furthermore, I will tell you what it is like to experience adventure unlike anything you could imagine.

My name is Adam and I will be your host as we journey through some of the first events in the history of mankind. Adam is the Hebrew word to describe a male individual or mankind in general. Since I am the first human created and am of the male gender, the name is fitting. Unlike you, I was created as a fully-grown adult. You were born as an infant and grew into adulthood. People always debate about which came first the chicken or the egg. I can tell you based on first-hand experience

-- it was the chicken. We were created on the same day out of the same material. The chicken was first, then me.

After creating everything He was going to create, God took some dirt from the ground, which He had already created, formed a human body (that would be me), and breathed life into it. God created me with intellect, the ability to think, emotion, the ability to express myself, and will, the ability to choose between various options. As a person, God gave me a material body with some immaterial parts. The material is that which you can see, feel, and touch. The immaterial is that which you cannot see, feel, or touch. The immaterial includes the soul, spirit, emotion, mind, conscience, will, and heart (not the organ).

I have never seen God. We talk but I only hear His movement and His voice. He is spirit. No one can see Him. He is a person with the characteristics of personhood. He has a name as well as intellect, emotion, and will. He created me in His own image and likeness. That can be puzzling. Since He is immaterial, and I am material, how is it that I am created in His own image and likeness? I have thought this through and concluded that it is a matter of relationship. Both of us have the ability to rationalize. God has already utilized His will in the creation process. He desires a relationship with me. I have the capacity to exercise my will to choose to have a relationship with Him. In that relationship I am morally capable of maintaining the innocence God created me with and physically capable of living forever in that relationship.

That is how I came into existence. He placed me in a beautiful friendly environment referred to as the Garden of Eden. My job was to tend to the garden. That wasn't hard. Everything was perfect. It had its own irrigation system. Water would come up from the ground periodically to keep the plants and trees properly hydrated, as well as to aid new growth which would spring forth. God did not overlook any detail in His creative plan. It was perfect.

There was a river in the garden with four tributaries. In the river were fish of all varieties, some large, some small. The largest of the sea creatures was called Leviathan and the largest land creature was Behemoth. They were majestic creatures. There was ample room in the garden for all of us to live and prosper.

One-day God took me aside and gave me one simple instruction. He said, "Do you see all these trees? You may eat the fruit of each one. This one is the Tree of Life. Its fruit has special properties fortifying the body to live forever. This tree is the Tree of the Knowledge of Good and Evil. Do not eat the fruit of this tree, for in the day you eat of it you will surely die."

I was a little confused because I didn't know what evil was nor did I know what it meant to die. I guess it was a matter of trust. I didn't need to know about evil and death just as long as I trust Him. He knows what is best for me. He knows everything. There should be no questions.

Part of tending the garden entails the naming of all the animals. All day long the different species come to me for a name. There seem to be multitude of them. This is going to take some time. All of these animals are herbivores. God gave them every green plant for food. I too am an herbivore.

God not only gave me the task of naming the animals, but He also gave me dominion over them. Whereas, I was created with intellect, emotion, and will, the animals were not created to think rationally. They react to the stimulus around them. He brought them to me and I gave each one a name.

There was no one but me. The animals had each other but I had no one like me to whom I could interact. It is true that God and I communicated with each other, but that was just his words to my ears. I longed for someone like myself to communicate with. Then came the day when God put me in a deep sleep. When I awoke there was someone like me in the sense that we both had similar flesh and bones, but there was a distinct difference in physicality. I referred to her as woman because her immaterial aspects were like mine, but her material aspects were very different. God had made us to complement each other. I called her woman because she was taken out of man. The two of us, though separate individuals, were to become one unit never to be divided.

The climate was perfect in the garden. The temperature was not too warm nor too cold. There was no need for clothing and the woman and I thought nothing of it. We went about tending to our daily duties working together to accomplish what God desired for us to do.

One afternoon we were walking in the garden, when suddenly and without notice, we were confronted by a creature right in front of the Tree of the Knowledge of Good and Evil. We had not encountered this species previously. Even I couldn't remember giving him a name. He spoke to the woman in a condescending tone, "Did God actually say you could not eat from any of the trees in the garden?"

The woman did not find it unusual for this creature to speak. She hastily answered, "We may eat of the fruit of any of the trees in the garden, but God did say we cannot eat from the tree that is in the midst of the garden or touch it lest we die." The tree in the midst of the garden was the Tree of the Knowledge of Good and Evil. I remember thinking, "Why did she say not to touch it? God didn't say that. I should know what He said, because He said it to me. She wasn't even created when God and I had that conversation." But I just stood there and let the two of them continue their dialog.

The creature answered, "You will not surely die. God knows that when you eat of the fruit of that tree your eyes will be open and you will be like Him, knowing good and evil." The woman, looking a little confused, stared at the tree in front of her. Something was happening. We had walked past that tree many times. What was she thinking? She later confided in me that the tree looked different than before. The fruit looked good as a food source, was aesthetically pleasing, and was promising as a means of wisdom. She reached up, put her hands around the fruit, plucked it from the branch, raised it to her mouth, and took a bite. Then she offered it to me. Well, nothing happened to her immediately, so I took a bite as well.

All hell broke loose. The creature was delighted. The woman and I looked at each other differently. Our nakedness became a problem. I didn't want her to see me. We tried to hide our nakedness. When we heard that familiar sound of God walking in the garden, we hid, so that He would not see us naked. But He called out, "Adam, where are you?" I was aware that He knew exactly where we were. I answered, "When I heard You coming in our direction, I became afraid and didn't want You to see me naked, so I hid from You.

His voice boomed, "Who told you that you were naked? Have you eaten from the tree I told you not to eat?"

I immediately went into a defensive mode. "The woman You gave me ate the fruit and then gave it to me. She is primarily responsible. You gave the woman to me, so you have some guilt as well."

He looked at the woman and in a thunderous voice said, "Do you realize what you have done?" She looked at Him and cried out, "The creature, he deceived me." Neither of us wanted to take responsibility for our actions. It was easier to blame someone else.

God looked at the creature and said, "Because you have done this, you shall be cursed to crawl on your belly and eat dust for the rest of your life. I will send a savior through the seed of the woman. You shall try to destroy Him, but He will destroy you." The creature which had been upright was now slithering along the dirt unable to return to his previous upright position.

God spoke to the woman, "You will bear children in pain and your desire will be to control your husband, but he will control you."

There was silence for a few seconds, which seemed like an eternity.

Finally, the irritation in His voice turned to disappointment as He directed His words toward me. He said, "Because you have believed the lie of the creature rather than the truth, the ground shall be cursed so that it will produce weeds along with wheat. You will be forced to exert all your effort in order to grow your own crops. I fashioned you from the dust of the earth. From dust you came and to dust you will go."

Then the worst came. God told me if I ate from the fruit of that tree I would surely die. I didn't die or, so I thought. But what did occur was an immediate separation. My fellowship that I enjoyed each day was now strained. The image and likeness of God in which I was created was now distorted. Everything was changed. The woman and I were banished from the garden and the Tree of Life. Although still alive, we were in the process of dying.

Starting a new life, I named the woman Eve because she would become the mother of all the living. The two of us were now in a hostile environment. Some time went by and Eve delivered a son. We named him Cain. Soon after that another son was born, Abel, as well as daughters. When Cain was old enough and the daughters were of childbearing age, they married and produced more offspring. Abel married and also produced offspring.

The boys were competitive and vied for attention. Being the firstborn, Cain seemed to be more intense than Abel. Cain was a farmer and Abel was a shepherd. Periodically, they brought offerings to the Lord. Cain brought the fruit of his crops and Abel brought the firstborn of his flock. On one occasion they made their offering to the Lord. Abel's sacrifice was acceptable, but Cain's was not. Cain was devastated. The Lord asked him why he was so downcast about it. Cain did not answer. The Lord said, "If you do the right thing for the right reason your conscience will react accordingly. However, we both know that is not true of you in this case." The next day Cain lured Abel out into the countryside and killed him in an act of jealousy. Trying to hide his crime, he dug a hole in the ground and buried him.

Cain went back to his farming tasks. The Lord said to him, "Where is Abel?" Cain answered sarcastically, "Am I now responsible for my brother's activities?" The Lord responded, "What have you done? Your brother's blood calls out to me. You are cursed. A fugitive you shall be, wandering around from place to place. The soil you work for your crops will rebel against you. Did you think I wouldn't find out what you had done?"

Cain answered, "I can't bear this punishment. You are taking my livelihood from me. You are taking your presence from me. I can no longer have a permanent location to call home. People will hunt me down and kill me."

The Lord answered, "No! I will put a mark on you. People will know that anyone who kills Cain will pay seven times for their action. The mark of Cain will keep you from vengeance."

Cain left the area with his wife and unmarried children. His firstborn was Enoch. His name means "initiation." The first village Cain settled he named after Enoch. How appropriate to symbolize the first abode of your new start, "initiation." Whether that start is good or bad, it is new.

Abel's death hit Eve and me hard. We lost Abel, and we lost Cain as well. We realized that our not believing God had serious repercussions. Not only did Abel have to lose his life but every person entering the world now carries the sin of Adam. Eve may have taken the first bite of the fruit, but God held me responsible. One mistake caused all this to occur. The innocence in which I was created has ebbed away.

Years passed by. Abel's sons and daughters continued to procreate. Eve bore other daughters who procreated. Grandchildren, great-grandchildren, and great great-grandchildren were abundant. The population was growing. Life was filled with discovery. It had to be that way. We were experiencing life for the first time. We had no precedents to follow. We were establishing them. Farming implements, metalcraft, and instruments of entertainment were just the beginning stages of what was yet to be developed.

There was another component to life that was not frequently discussed and remained stagnant. The relationship Eve and I had with God in the Garden was barely alive. Eve vividly recalled those days and wanted to reignite the fire within our hearts, but there wasn't much enthusiasm for the idea.

I had been alive for one hundred and thirty years and fathered two boys who were no longer with me. Eve became pregnant and was delighted to give birth to another male child. She was insistent that this child was appointed to take Abel's place, so we named him Seth which means "placed." Those spiritual matters that Eve was so hopeful for gradually began to change. It took one hundred and five years to be exact. It was then that Seth fathered Enosh and people began calling on the name of the Lord. It only took two hundred and thirty-five years.

God created me in His image and likeness. Seth was born in my image and likeness, reflecting the sin that was counted against everyone born after Eve and I ate the fruit of the forbidden tree.

As the patriarch, it was incumbent on me to keep exact records of births and deaths. I developed a chart that would chronicle the birth, lifespan, and death of each successive generation. On the chart were recorded the births of Seth through Lamech. As I aged and came closer to my time on earth being over, I handed off that responsibility to Methuselah.

An interesting thing happened in the seventh generation. Enoch was born to Jared. There was something special about him. We talked, especially as I got older. He had a really strong relationship with God. It seemed as though his relationship evolved after the birth of Methuselah. Maybe it was the father-son relationship that caused him to take a more serious attitude about spiritual matters. I don't know. But what I do know is that he lived his life as though God was his first priority. By all rights I should have been a role model for him. In reality he was my role model. Pay close attention to his life for he is on the right path.

That's about it for me. I've given you all the information I have at present. If you are still interested in learning more, see what Methuselah has to say. I've turned all the responsibility over to him.

Chapter Two

His Death Shall Bring Judgment

L et's start from the very beginning. Once there was nothing. Out of that nothingness came something. "How can that be," you ask? Well logic demands at least two options. Option one would be spontaneous generation. That simply means it just happened. There is no explanation except for the fact that the world exists, and I am part of it. The second option is that an entity outside of the natural world conceptualized, designed, and created everything in existence both visible and invisible.

Over nine hundred years ago my ancestor, Adam, answered that question. He actually talked with the designer and creator on a daily basis, until a rather unfortunate choice was made to ignore the wise counsel of the Creator, opting instead to heed the advice of a creature, who not only was not looking out for the best interest of Adam, but in fact wanted to destroy him. Whew! That was a lengthy sentence. Nevertheless, an important one, because it contrasts the gibberish of spontaneity with the necessity of an Ultimate Reality.

You are familiar with the story. God created Adam and Eve and placed them in the Garden of Eden. He issued only one prohibition to test them. "Do not eat of the tree in the midst of the garden." Unfortunately, they failed the test and were exiled from the garden after which, they had two male children, Cain and Abel. Out of jealousy Cain killed Abel. Because of his foul deed, God cursed Cain to be a nomad, wandering from place to place. Cain and his offspring moved away from Adam and Eve and continued a lifestyle of rebellion against God. His offspring seemed to share his rebellious attitude. They were inventive, being both boisterous and boastful, trying to outdo the evil in each other.

Meanwhile, the other side of the family was increasing biologically. Spiritual growth was stagnant at best for one hundred and thirty years. Adam fathered Seth in his own image and likeness. A distorted image from the original. Eve was pleased to have given birth to a male child to replace Abel. Spiritual growth was trending positively but not at the pace Eve desired. It would be an additional one hundred and five years before people in general began to call upon the name of the Lord.

My name is Methuselah and I have been tasked with the responsibility of continuing to chronicle the development of the family tree. My ancestor Adam started the process in more ways than one. He was the first of creation and the first to record the lineage. At the age of nine hundred and thirty, as he was close to death, he placed the charts of the family in my hands and officially appointed me to be the family historian. He had successfully recorded eight generations of births. As is usually the case, he predeceased his offspring after Seth. I often wondered why he chose me as the family scribe. It took me fifty-seven years to figure it out. This is my story.

The chart below is what Adam gave to me just before he died. The time was nine hundred and thirty years after God breathed life into Adam. His chronological chart consisted of a column with the name of the individual, the year they were born, the year they died, and their age at death

Family Chronology

Name	Year born	Year Died	Age at Death
Adam	1	930	930
Seth	130		
Enosh	235		
Cainan	325		
Mahalel	395		
Jared	460		
Enoch	622		
Methuselah	687		
Lamech	874		

It was up to me to fill in the chart from this point. What I discovered was most interesting. Below is the chart completed to the year 1056.

Family Chronology

Name	Year Born	Year Died	Age at Death
Adam	1	930	930
Seth	130	1042	912
Enosh	235	1050	815
Cainan	325	1235	910
Mahalel	395	1290	895
Jared	460	1422	962
Enoch	622		
Methuselah	687		
Lamech	874	1651	777
Noah	1056		

Notice that by that year there are only three recorded names that do not show a date of death, my father Enoch, me, and my grandson Noah. All three of us had a role to play in the drama that was to unfold.

My father, Enoch, was a good man by human standards. For the first sixty-five years of his life there is nothing to suggest that he did anything other than what any other man of his era would have done. But in his sixty-fifth year a change took place. My mother says it was both immediate and gradual. It was immediate in that she could see there was something different about him and it was gradual in that he continued to evolve from the ordinary to the extraordinary.

From the time I was old enough to pay attention to someone other than myself, I followed in my dad's footsteps. Just as he followed in the footsteps of God, I followed in his. It wasn't just me. My brothers and sisters as well as the whole community watched with awe as dad lived his life like he really believed what he said. There was no guile or hypocrisy found in him. His life was as refreshing as a cup of cool water in the heat of the desert sun. I'm not saying he was perfect. No one is. But he set an example for all of us to follow.

Three hundred years of walking with the Lord will prepare you for something special; that's how long after I was born that it happened. We had just celebrated my three hundredth birthday. My brothers and sisters were all there as well as other guests. Dad was in a particularly jovial mood. We gathered around the table for a meal when Dad began walking toward the desert. It looked and sounded as though he was carrying on a conversation with someone. We called out to him, but he did not respond. He kept walking. We called out again. He turned toward us as if to say something. He smiled, waved his hand, and was gone. He disappeared like a mirage in the desert. We rushed to where we last saw him, but he wasn't there. One minute he was walking and in an instant, he was no more.

No one had a reasonable explanation as to what had happened. We didn't know what to expect next. If we had not witnessed it firsthand, we might have thought someone, or something had either abducted him or worse than that killed him and buried the body. But we knew better. What we didn't know was how or what had happened.

Time went by and Dad did not return. After much discussion we concluded that while on earth Dad walked symbolically with the Lord. The only viable explanation was that now he was literally walking with the Lord. No one disappears from sight in front of many witnesses without supernatural help. God, Who he so faithfully served, spared him from physical death and took him to be with Him eternally. His name, Enoch, means "dedicated." He truly was dedicated to the God of the universe. He was a prophet in more ways than one. A prophet communicates what God wants to convey to humankind. He speaks for God. As a preacher of righteousness, Dad warned people about upcoming judgment. How the Lord was coming with ten thousand angels to mete out justice and convict all of their ungodly deeds as well as the blasphemy they had committed against Him.

Sometimes a testimony is more powerful when no words are spoken. More often than not actions speak louder than words. Adam died but Dad lived. Everyone else eventually died. Despite death coming into existence due to Adam's sin, God, sparing Dad from physical death, was a clear sign that there is a way that leads to hope. Walking with God, trusting Him, believing that He knows what is best was the message of hope communicated to mankind by God through His prophet, Enoch.

My story doesn't end there. I still have six hundred sixty-nine years left to live. How do I know that? Keep reading and you will see.

The population is quickly increasing. One reason is the average lifespan. Just look at the family chronological chart. The average is eight hundred eighty-five years. The combination of new births and long lifespan continue to rapidly edge the population in an upward progression. Even the role model Dad provided could not possibly be experienced by such a large population. As a matter of fact, moral evil has accelerated so much that every intention of man is evil. I don't see how matters can get much worse.

But as more time goes by things are indeed getting much worse. Men possessed by demons are marrying any and all the women they can, without restraint. Children who are born out of this malicious wedlock are just as evil if not more so than their heathen parents. Something needs to be done about this atrocious situation.

God created Adam with the ability to make choices. The first choice he made was catastrophic, bringing death into the world. A spiritual and physical separation occurred and the innocence in which he was created was lost. Evil has supplanted innocence, affecting the choices people are making. The immaterial part of man called the conscience has been so seared by evil that man's heart has become the most devious. The hounds of hell have been unleashed. Things surely couldn't get any worse. But they did.

In the year 1056 my grandson Noah was born. He is a determined young man. A man of prayer. When he was five hundred years old he fathered Japheth. Two years later he fathered Shem. Lastly, he fathered Ham. The family lived among the vilest people that ever inhabited the earth. Circumstances were so bad that God regretted having made them in the first place. Now it should be pointed out that God knew what would happen, but that did not negate His disappointment. Noah found favor in the eyes of the Lord. The Lord said to him, "Mankind has become so evil that I have determined to destroy all flesh. I want you to build an ark. The dimensions shall be four hundred fifty feet long, seventy-five feet wide, and forty-five feet high. It is to have three floors inside and a roof one and one-half feet above the third floor. Seal it with tar to make it waterproof. Construct a door in the side of the ark for entrance and exit. I will pour out My wrath on all flesh by bringing a flood over the whole earth. I will spare you, your wife, and your sons and their wives.

As you are building the ark, you are to preach to the people with whom you come into contact. It will take you one hundred and twenty years to build the ark. The people will not listen to you and will persecute you. Pay no attention to them. Just keep preaching and building.

When you have finished the building, call the animals to come to you both male and female. Take two of each species along with an abundant supply of food into the ark.

Because we were so close, Noah shared the Lord's words to him with me. We had many conversations about how the Lord would accomplish the judgment he was to bring upon all mankind, young and old alike. It grieved both of us to think of all the life that would be lost.

Noah did as he was told. His neighbors and all who heard about his project chided Him. But his determination kept his hand to the task, despite the difficulties. Finally, the day came when the ark was complete. Prior to Noah calling the animals, I handed the task of keeping the family records to him. It was my nine hundredth and sixty ninth year of life. A life lived to the full as the oldest to ever have lived and the only one whose life spanned the generations from Adam to Noah. Lamech had died five years earlier, making Noah and me the only surviving heads of the family. I perceived it was my time to experience the afterlife. Either God would spare me from physical death as He did my father, or I would die from natural causes prior to God pouring out His wrath. My father named me Methuselah. Names have meanings. My name means "His death shall bring judgment." If you want to know more, listen to my grandson, Noah. He will give you more details.

Chapter Three

Judgment

I'm proud to say that my grandfather was the oldest man in recorded history. During his nine hundred and sixty-nine years, he was able to talk with Adam and learned from him the highs of the Garden of Eden and the lows of being expelled from there. He saw firsthand the godly way his father conducted his life; a life that was honored by the Lord when he preserved him from physical death. Both his father, Enoch, and his son, Lamech were prophets. His father warned of judgment and his son spoke of the restoration that would come. The name my father Lamech, gave me, Noah, means "rest." Surrounded by such greatness, is it any wonder that God spared him the coming judgment. After all his name, Methuselah means "After he dies, judgment." Indeed, that is what happened. In the one thousand six hundred and fifty sixth year after creation, I buried my grandfather. The events leading up to that day and what happened thereafter will be contained in this report, for prior to his death, he commissioned me to be the family scribe, responsible for maintaining historical records.

Long lifespans were the norm for me growing up. My father, Lamech, was the youngest of the pre-flood patriarchs to die He was seven hundred seventy-seven years old. It was a day of decadence and an age of antipathy. The starting point can be traced back to before the foundation of the world.

Prior to God creating the physical world, He created magnificent creatures known as sons of God and morning stars. These were immaterial beings created for the benefit of those who would inherit salvation. Among these two categories were the cherub, the seraph, and the watcher. These creatures were arranged in a hierarchy with an archangel, sometimes called a chief prince, as the leader. Each were given attributes of personhood. They had a name, intellect, emotion, and will. All were created at the same time. They do not procreate, nor do they die. There will never be any more or any fewer of them.

Three of these creatures stand out. All three were given leadership roles among their peers. Michael was given the task of being a chief prince, Gabriel was to be the messenger, and Helel was to be the worship leader.

Like everything else God created, these immaterial beings, now called angels, were perfect. There was nothing outside of them to tempt them in any way to go off course. They were given the ability to think, react to stimulus, and to make choices. Helel became disenchanted with his role as worship leader. He wanted to be God. His pride overtook him, and he sinned. As a result, God cast him out of heaven. He was not without influence as one third of the angels followed him in his sin. He became an adversary of God and made it his goal to battle God continuously for the souls of mankind. Instead of being Helel, son of dawn, he became Satan, the adversary. His fate along with all those who followed him was sealed. There was not then, nor will there ever be, an opportunity for repentance.

Since that fatal decision, Satan has made it his goal to crouch at the door, waiting for unsuspecting persons to pounce on, in order to destroy them. He became the leader of the hierarchy of unholy angels sometimes called, powers, rulers, principalities, demons, and unclean spirits. As their leader, Satan is known as Beelzebub, Lord of the Flies.

In the Garden of Eden, Satan possessed a serpent and tricked Eve into eating fruit from the tree which God had commanded Adam not to eat. After taking a bite of the fruit, she offered Adam a bite. He also ate from the fruit. As a result, sin entered the world. Innocence was forfeited, and death was the result. Satan and his workers of evil have been busy ever since trying to negatively influence humankind.

All of my life I have observed this battle between God and Satan. The effects of the battle are everywhere apparent. As I look back over the nine hundred and fifty years of my life I can see Satan operating in various ways.

When my father named me, I became a child of promise. Noah means "rest." Dad prophesied about me, saying "Out of the ground that the Lord has cursed this one shall bring us relief from our work and from the painful toil of our hands." Living under the shadow of two prophets can be a daunting experience. It clearly gave me a different perspective than my contemporaries.

Every generation thinks the succeeding generation is getting worse behaviorally. It is commonplace to hear someone say, "These kids today need more discipline. Why in my day we would never get by doing what they do today." Memory is oftentimes selective. But in this case the old-timers were right. Conditions were getting increasingly worse. Some of the unholy angels had actually left their own abode to take up residence in men. That's right, demons possessed humans. Just like Satan controlled the serpent in the Garden of Eden, these unholy angels dominated the thoughts and actions of men, some of whom were my relatives. No amount of preaching or prophesying could change their mindset. The more we preached against the evil of the day, the harder the demons pushed for their own agenda. Violence was rampant. People would intentionally harm one another, even to the point of senseless murder. If someone wanted something you had, they would just take it. The sons of God would manipulate men to take as many wives as they wanted. Whatever evil the mind could envision would be carried out. Evil thoughts initiated evil actions.

Philosophers justified the evil actions by blaming God for giving man the ability to choose. They would say, "If God had not given man the ability to choose, we would not be in this situation." Others blamed Satan saying, "The Devil made me do it." Still others said, "If there is a God, the judgment you preach about would have already taken place. But nothing has changed, and nothing will change. Life is to be enjoyed any way one wants to live. Everyone has the right to freedom of thought and action. You do your thing and I'll do mine." There was no accountability. No responsibility. It was a no-fault, take all you can get, look out for number one kind of world.

Because of the role models I had, spiritual matters were important to me. I became dependent on prayer just to get through life's daily struggles. I patterned my spiritual life after my dad, granddad, and great granddad. They taught me how to walk with the Lord. As a result of being close to the Lord, He made it clear to us that His Spirit would not tolerate the evil exhibited in the flesh that was in the world. He set a time limit of one hundred twenty years. Then he would destroy all flesh and blot it out from the face of the earth. One day in the year fifteen hundred thirty-six He spoke to me personally, saying "Noah, you have found favor in my eyes. I am going to destroy all flesh on the earth. I want you to build a huge boat as a sanctuary for you, your wife, your sons, and their wives."

Even though the population was exploding, my wife and I had not yet brought children into the world. I'm not sure if we ever consciously talked about it. The atmosphere was just not right. I think we probably ignored the obvious. But here God was telling me He would not only save me and my wife, but He would save three sons who were yet unborn and their wives. I was astounded by what He said yet I had learned over the past four hundred eighty years to trust whatever He said because it was truth.

He gave me specific instructions on the dimensions of the boat, the interior design, and the materials He wanted me to use. My first thought was, "This is a big boat." That thought was interrupted when He told me He wanted me to call all the different species of animals and select a male and female from each species to take on the boat with us. In addition, I was to take a supply of green plants for food for both humans and animals. I realized this would be a plan of epic proportions.

During this time, I had many discussions with my grandfather. He wanted to make sure I remained humble during this entire experience. How easy it would have been to let my ego get in the way of a truly miraculous event, to forget the grace given to me so undeservedly, to think I was someone special. I needed to be constantly reminded not to be wise in my own opinion.

Twenty years after the Lord spoke to me about the judgment He was to bring on the earth, and how the ark I was building would be used to save me, my wife, my sons, and their wives, my first son, Japheth, was born. Two years later my second son, Shem, was born. Finally, Ham was born. This would complete my family.

As the Lord directed me, I began to gather the materials and drafted the plan for the ark. Passersby would invariably inquire as to what I was doing. This gave me the opportunity to speak to them about the coming judgment. Most of the people walked away thinking I had lost my mind. Some made crude remarks, while others broke out in laughter. The comments they made were not what you would want your young children to hear about their father. When the boys came to me asking why these people were so mean, I would take the time to explain how people should treat each other with respect. They accepted my explanation based on trust when they were young. As they matured, Methuselah told them stories about Adam and Enoch which strengthened their resolve.

The times were hard to deal with. The ark was in various stages of development over the one hundred and twenty years. It was a constant reminder of the faith and trust our family placed in God. It was also a constant reminder of the judgment that was to come. Many tears were shed knowing that our friends, neighbors, and relatives would be facing the wrath of God. Yes, brothers, sisters, aunts, uncles, and cousins who chose not to trust in the Lord would face destruction. Adults as well as children would perish in the worst disaster in human history. All of that was very real to us every day.

The boys grew and began looking for wives. Fathers were unwilling for their daughters to marry people they thought were unstable, and that is what they thought about our entire family. Brides were eventually found for all three boys despite the bias against us. Time continued to grow short.

The day came when the ark was complete. It was time to call the animals. People were astounded to see all the livestock, beasts of the field, birds of the air, and every creeping species marching toward the ark. Two of each species, male and female, boarded the ark. There were horses, cows, sheep, lions, bears, dinosaurs, giraffes, monkeys, eagles, serpents, and hippopotamus just to name a few. It was a visit to the zoo in reverse. Instead of going to see the wildlife, the wildlife came to see us. Such an unusual scene should have sparked questions in the minds of the people who witnessed this amazing animal roundup. But it did not. People were so enamored with their lifestyle that nothing really affected them.

Methuselah witnessed the drawing of the animals. I spoke with him just before they came. He was nine hundred sixty-nine years old. As a supreme optimist, he was hopeful the march of the animals would persuade people to repent. But it did not. I think he died from a broken heart. All I really know is that the floodwaters didn't take his life. He slept with the fathers before the door of the ark was closed. Now I was the family patriarch.

In the six hundredth year of my life, on the tenth day of the second month, sixteen hundred fifty-six years after the creation, I heard the Lord invite me to come into the ark; the ark I had built at His direction. The sanctuary that would save the lives of my family. I entered the ark with my wife, my sons, and my son's wives amidst the presence of the Lord, who shut the door and sealed us safely inside.

Seven days passed. On the seventeenth day of the month, rain began to fall. It would continue that way for forty days and forty nights. Adam shared with Methuselah, that God told him when He created the universe, there were two reservoirs of water. One was under the great expanse, referring to the water of the great deep, and the other was over the great expanse, referring to the windows of heaven. Water violently erupted from the great deep, and viciously cascaded from the windows of heaven. It was a shock and awe moment as the waters battered against the ark, causing it to float almost immediately. The ark was massive, but the turbulent waters dictated the course the vessel would take.

There was a heart sickening, gut wrenching, cry heard from the people the ark left behind. They were trying to get to higher ground in order to keep from drowning. But it would be to no avail as the floodwaters rose over the mountaintops by twenty-two feet. All the flesh of men and animals were destroyed. Every living thing on earth was blotted out. Only the occupants of the ark prevailed. The floodwaters began to subside after one hundred fifty days.

Life on the ark was solemn. There were times when the thunder boomed, and the lightning flashed with such intensity that it seemed as though no one would make it through the ordeal. The turbulent water and high waves caused the ark to bob up and down and side to side with nauseating force. There was nowhere to go that the smell of the animals did not permeate the air.

The waters maintained a depth of twenty-two feet over the mountains for one hundred and fifty days. God called to a halt the eruption of the deep, closed the windows of heaven, and caused a wind to blow across the water filled land. The waters began to recede. On the first day of the tenth month the mountain peaks could be seen. The ark came to rest on Mount Ararat. Day by day the waters continued to recede. Forty days went by. All of us were getting restless. The animals were getting restless. As spacious as the ark was, it felt like the walls were hemming us in.

I waited forty days and released a raven to try and determine whether it was safe to disembark the boat and release the animals. It flew back and forth and was little help in determining the condition of the land. I released a dove, hoping she would find some evidence of land. The dove came back. I waited seven days and sent out another dove. This one returned with an olive leaf in her beak, indicating the land had reappeared. I waited another seven days and released another dove. This one did not return. It was the first day of the first month of the six hundred and first year of my time on earth. We knew the water had receded completely, but earth wasn't ready for us just yet. On the twenty seventh day of the second month in my six hundred and first year, God spoke to me saying, "The time has come for you and your family to leave the ark, release the animals, and begin to repopulate the earth." From the time we entered the ark until the time we disembarked was three hundred seventy-seven days.

The door had been sealed and God had shut us in when we boarded the ark. In the same way, He opened the door for us that we could disembark. I learned that when God closes one door, He opens another. As we began our walk down the ramp to the dry ground, we were celebrating. Even though we were in the mountains, we were grateful, first of all, because we were safe, and secondly because we were out of that boat.

The animals were just as anxious to be set free. The way the animals entered the ark was systematic and organized. The exit from the ark was fast and furious. Something had changed with the animals. No longer did they tarry around us. They ran from us. They ran from each other. Some of the animals grazed while other larger animals began to stalk some of the smaller animals.

The Lord spoke to me. He said, "Things have changed. Before, you were restricted to eating every plant yielding seed and the fruit of the trees. Now, every moving thing that lives shall be food for you. The only restriction is that you must not consume the blood. You were an herbivore, but now you are a carnivore. Henceforth, the beasts of the field, the birds of the air, and all that creeps on the ground will live in fear of you. Likewise, the animals will no longer be restricted to the green plants. They too will be carnivores. But I will require an accounting from any man or animal that spills the blood of man. For if one sheds the blood of man by man his blood shall be shed."

All of us on the ark had been through a traumatic experience. We were alive but carried with us the reality of death. We all were familiar with the death of a loved one, but to encounter death on a wholesale basis shocked us to the very core of our being. God knew the frailty of our hearts. He spoke to us in a reassuring manner saying, "This day I am establishing an everlasting covenant with you and every living creature that survived the flood judgment. Never again will I destroy the earth by water. As a sign of the covenant to every living creature, I am placing a rainbow in the clouds as a remembrance." Then there appeared in the clouds a multicolored arc consisting of seven bands, i.e. red, orange, yellow, green, blue, indigo, and violet.

God continued, "Be fruitful and multiply. Fill the earth." I knew he was speaking to the boys, for my wife and I were well beyond child bearing age. We descended Mount Ararat to the valley below. Two rivers formed a border to a fertile land we called Mesopotamia. The two rivers flowed from the mountains and emptied into a larger body of water considerably farther south. It was there that we made our first home. There is more to tell, but now is not the time. We must first busy ourselves in the work of starting over.

Chapter Four

Rest

There was plenty of work to be done. Rebuilding a civilization takes time. First is the task of making a base of operations. The boys and I scouted the area for a cave that would be suitable for temporary living. The floodwaters destroyed everything, and the silt covered up the remnants of any building materials. We gathered wood for a fire and kept the domestic animals in close proximity. Remember, there was only a male and female of each species. Camels and donkeys were used for transportation and goats for milk. It was now permissible to eat the flesh of the animals, but it wasn't very wise and would have defeated the purpose of bringing them on the ark. Time had to pass allowing for the animal kingdom to repopulate.

The gestation period for large mammals (cows, horses, donkeys, camels) is approximately three hundred sixty days. For small mammals (sheep and goats), the gestation period is approximately one hundred fifty days. These are considered domestic animals. For the most part these animals eat grain and grass. The lion, tiger, and wolf are aggressive meat eaters. The gestation period for the wolf is approximately sixty days. The lion and tiger have a gestation period of approximately one hundred eight days. It takes less time to birth the aggressive carnivore than it does to birth the domestic herbivore. In addition, the aggressive carnivore has more cubs and pups at one time than the larger mammals.

Some provisions were still left from the ark but not that much. There were, however, an abundance of seeds. There were olive seeds for oil, dates, figs, pomegranates, wheat, barley, and leeks. The ground was fertile, but all these plants did not grow at the same time. A garden would need to be planted and reaped during the appropriate seasons. Like I said, there is nothing easy about rebuilding a civilization.

Let me give you an idea of the challenges we face. A goat can produce one gallon of milk per day, while a camel can produce up to eight gallons of milk per day. A goat produces up to sixteen pounds of hair per year, while a camel produces up to five pounds of hair per year. It will take at least fifteen months for the male and female goats we took on board to have a flock of sixteen goats. Between the goats and the camels there will be enough milk to drink and hair to make tents for the eight of us to shelter under.

It takes three years for olives and grapes to be viable. Dates take four to eight years. Pomegranates take two to three years. Leeks take eight to ten weeks. Wheat and barley take sixty to seventy days. I share all of this with you so that you might understand that building a civilization takes time. It can get frustrating.

Here is a glimpse at what frustration looks like. I made a decision to plant a vineyard. Grapes have always been plentiful, and the juice of the grape is pleasant to the taste. As a general rule, a grapevine will produce fruit in the third season. I know all these things because I am a farmer. After harvesting the grapes, I decided to let some of them ferment into wine. One night I drank more than I should of the intoxicating beverage. It was especially hot that night, so I removed my robe in the privacy of my tent. The wine made me sleepy and I passed out on my bed. Ham came into my tent and saw me. He immediately went to his brothers and gleefully told them what he had seen. Shem and Japheth came to my tent, took my garment, and covered me up. They did not look upon my nakedness, as Ham had done.

Ham disrespected me. As a consequence, I prophesied against him, "Cursed be your son, Canaan. He will be a servant to Shem and Japheth."

Shem, Ham, and Japheth fathered sons and daughters just as the Lord commanded. My wife and I were elderly and beyond child bearing age. The population began to grow. Two years after the flood, when Shem was one hundred years old, a son, Arpachshad, was born. He was one of five sons fathered by Shem. I continued recording the data of the family chronology that Adam started. Below are the entries as of the two thousandth year of creation.

Name	Year Born	Year Died	Age at Death
Adam	1	930	930
Seth	130	1042	912
Enosh	235	1050	815
Cainan	325	1235	910

Mahalel	395	1290	895
Jared	460	1422	962
Enoch	622		
Methuselah	687	1656	969
Lamech	874	1651	777
Noah	1056		
Shem	1558		
Flood	1656		
Arpachshad	1658		
Salah	1693		
Eber	1723		
Peleg	1757	1996	239
Reu	1787		
Serug	1819		
Nahor	1849	1997	148
Terah	1878		

You might ask, "Why is the line of Shem the only chronology that was kept?" Ham was eliminated due to the curse placed upon his descendants. The Lord revealed to me that Japheth and his descendants would benefit spiritually from Shem and his descendants. Ham and Japheth's genealogies were preserved but not the chronology. I didn't inquire of the Lord further regarding the matter. He is God and can do whatever He wishes without explaining His decisions to me.

Although an official chronology was not maintained for Ham and Japheth, there was information helpful for determining timelines. After the flood the average time frame of a generation was thirty-seven years. Ham fathered Cush in 1658. When Cush was thirty-seven years old he fathered Nimrod.

God's command to increase and multiply was being carried out. However, his command to fill the earth was not. People became comfortable and did not want to migrate to areas in which they were uncomfortable. Remember, outside of my sons and their offspring, there were no other people on earth.

Eventually, we migrated from the area of Mount Ararat to the plain called Shinar. It was located in what came to be known as the Fertile Crescent. The land was bounded by the Tigris and Euphrates Rivers. Nimrod became a mighty hunter. Since many animals were now carnivores, there was a need to defend ourselves from their attacks. For the most part the animals had a fear of humans, but there were some who preyed on flesh. Those with hunting skills were seen as protectors of the villages and towns. Nimrod fell into this category and became the first recognized leader. He began to spread out his influence by establishing communities within the Fertile Crescent. The first of these was Babel.

One hundred years after the flood a son was born to Eber in the line of Shem. His father named him Peleg. The name means "division." We didn't realize the significance of that name at the outset. But within a short period of time, we experienced the reality of the name. Nimrod was sixty-two years old when Peleg was born.

There was a certain rebelliousness with Nimrod. The attention and accolades he garnered from the townspeople seemed to enlarge his ego. He began to deviate from what was considered acceptable behavior to return to pre-flood attitudes. Satan found him to be a willing vessel to continue his battle with God. Instead of living in tents and expanding the horizons as God had instructed, Nimrod led the people to make bricks from the sand and seal them with the tar found abundantly in the area just under the surface of the earth. The tar was a thick gooey substance used as a binding and waterproofing agent.

A sharp contrast existed between Eber and Nimrod. Eber seemed compliant to God's will, but Nimrod was more interested in Nimrod. It wasn't as though Nimrod was an atheist. He was not. He believed in gods. He just didn't put all his eggs in one basket. There is a legend that says Nimrod built the tower in Babel and worshipped many gods. The most important god to him was himself.

There was one society, speaking one language, with one leader. The people feared they would be dispersed over the earth and didn't find that notion to be acceptable. They banded together at the instigation of Nimrod and developed a three-pronged plan. First, they decided to build a permanent civilization in the land of Shinar. The plan was to build a city. Second, they began building a tower. Their plan was to reach to the heavens. They sought a higher being and thought they could reach this being by their own ingenuity. Unfortunately, this being was a god but not The God. Third, the motivation for the construction was to make a name for themselves. They thought that if they stood together in solidarity they could impose their will over anyone or anything that challenged them. Much like Satan, Adam, and the sons of God, the people were not satisfied with their role in life and opted to follow their own will as opposed to heeding the command of God. Because of their pride and willful determination not to spread out, God confused their language, resulting in them not being able to understand each other. They were scattered over the face of the earth as a result.

Those that did understand each other settled lands together. The Hamites ventured to the southwest, the Japhethites settled to the coastal areas of the Great Sea, and the Shemites traveled west to the hill country. Some in each group traveled both east and west north and south.

The ones who remained in Babel continued their practice of serving false gods. The area became infested with demons. Every diabolic thought and idea that emanated from there was saturated with evil.

Babel was the first city founded by Nimrod. He also established cities in other locales. The tower built in Babel is known as "the house of Nimrod." The scattering of the people did not change Nimrod's behavior. He continued his downward spiritual spiral. I lost contact with him but the last I heard he had married a woman named Semiramus. She was as evil as he was. Legend has it that the two of them were celebrating the New Year. She requested that Nimrod make her the ruler for one day with all the rights and privileges of a king. Nimrod granted her that request whereupon, she promptly had him executed and assumed the throne.

During this same time period, another seismic event took place. Not only were the peoples dispersed but the earth was divided as well. The pressure from the eruption of the fountains from the deep finally took a toll on the land causing it to separate. Great expanses divided land masses and once verdant land became desert sand.

Families were separated. Shem and his descendants through Peleg's family became detached from Joktan and his family. Shem's descendants settled in Mesopotamia and lands west of where the ark rested. Joktan and his descendants settled in southwest Arabia.

As traumatic as the flood was, as difficult as establishing a new civilization was, there was always the hope of what is yet to come. That is still the case. The line of Shem is still producing sons and daughters. They have been affected by the evil influence of Nimrod and those that carry on his malevolent legacy.

When it was time for me to appoint a new family patriarch, I chose Eber. He was conscientious and was held in high esteem by those who knew him. Nine hundred and fifty years is a long time to live. I can't have too many days left. I've done what has been asked of me to the best of my ability. Now, I could finally enjoy the meaning of my name and rest in peace.

Chapter Five

The Region Beyond

Time marched on. It waited for no man. It seemed that God had forgotten us. People weren't living a long time as they had previously. Noah lived nine hundred fifty years. I was two hundred eighty-three years old when Noah died. He and I had many conversations about the ark, the flood, and the conditions that caused God to extend his judgment to all the earth. My name is Eber, and just like Adam, Methuselah, and Noah before me, I have been given the responsibility of chronicling the family history.

Seventeen hundred fifty-seven years from Adam's creation a significant event took place. My wife bore a son. We talked at length about naming the child. Since it was my responsibility to name him, I called him Peleg. The name means "division." It turned out to be prophetic for what was going to soon take place. Three significant events occurred during Peleg's lifetime.

The first event was the division of the earth. More than one hundred years after the flood, the earth's landscape was changed. People travelled far away and were forced to settle a new land far from that of the Fertile Crescent. When the land separated some families were immediately disconnected from the land of their youth and forced to colonize a new location a very long way from home. A great expanse of water appeared where a land mass had been.

The second event was the separation of people groups. Clans within the tribes of the sons of Noah were dispersed over the land.

Third was the separation of siblings. Joktan, Peleg's younger brother, and his sons settled the southern part of Arabia while the descendants of Peleg favored the southern part of Mesopotamia near the mouth of the Euphrates.

Shem was my great-grandfather. He was considered the patriarch of all the children born in my family. I was born sixty-seven years after the flood when Shem was one hundred sixty-five years old. Peleg was born when I was thirty-four. Joktan, Peleg's brother, was born after Peleg. The name Joktan means "less importance." Just as I named Peleg, I named Joktan as well. You might want to know why I gave a child a name meaning "less importance." It wasn't that I loved Peleg more than Joktan, or that I favored Peleg over Joktan. After all, Joktan had thirteen sons who settled the lands of Arabia. They were stout, hard working men. Sons in which a father could take pride. But there was something about Peleg that overshadowed Joktan, making him less in stature. Despite the meaning of the name, Joktan's significance was respected enough that he was included in the genealogy of Shem.

The population was growing rapidly, even though the average age of death for the line of Shem was about one third of the average pre-flood age.

Noah was our hero, our patriarch, revered more than any other man. A premier preacher and storyteller, he would regale us with anecdotes of how God would encourage him when he needed it most and exhort him when he least expected it. Selective memory was not a problem with Noah. His portrayal of the good, the bad, and the ugly of human existence was vividly exposed as he related his stories, designed to help us in our spiritual growth.

Although he was beloved, he had his detractors as well. Nimrod was especially critical of Noah's monotheistic beliefs. He preferred a pantheon of gods, a buffet of deity that could be chosen at will. The values the two men espoused were as different as night from day. Nimrod was selfish, driven by ego, while Noah was selfless, driven by a desire to serve the God in whom he placed his trust. Whenever someone mentioned Noah, Nimrod would find a way to denigrate that person.

So, the battle raged; good versus evil. That, according to Noah, was the reason for God taking the action of displacing the people from their comfort zones to fill the earth as He had commanded. The division of the land forced people to utilize the four corners of the earth as opposed to occupying only a portion of the land. If left unattended, the rebelliousness would only be the beginning of the evil to which they would resort.

Peleg fathered Rue, who fathered Serug, who fathered Nahor, who fathered Terah. One hundred and twenty-one years passed by. It seemed as though good was losing out. Nimrod's influence was so strong that false gods were being worshipped in the line of Shem. As Terah aged he worshipped Sin, the moon god. Sin was one of the forty-four gods in the Babylonian pantheon. He followed in importance the four major gods, An, Enlil, Inana, and Enki. So, you can see how far man had digressed as a result of Nimrod's influence.

Terah was the father of Abram, Nahor, and Haran. He was seventy years of age when Haran was born and one hundred thirty years of age when Abram was born. Haran died in Ur of the Chaldeans where Terah and Abram lived.

Nestled between the Euphrates River and the Lower Sea, the city served as an important commercial center, specializing in the importing and exporting of incense and silk. Religiously, the city boasted of a seventy-foot-tall ziggurat. Each section of the structure was a different color. The shrine was dedicated to the moon god as the chief deity. The monument was not the only area of false worship. Gods of all description were plentiful and available as a person saw fit to worship. This was the environment in which my great-great-great-great grandson Abram was born.

Abram was a shy person. He didn't want to draw attention to himself. He was always being confronted about something to the point where he seemed paranoid about people wanting to do him harm. As a young man he married a beautiful woman named Sarai. This woman was stunning, and Abram was forever worrying that someone would come along and take her from him.

We had many conversations. He always wanted to know about the great flood, and he could sit and listen for hours to what I told him Noah said to me. He always remarked that Noah must have really trusted his God to keep on building the ark against such mounting opposition. Over and over again he repeated to me this question, "Didn't it bother him that all those people made him the object of their ridicule?" I told him what Noah told me. "God offered me life with Him. How could I value anything greater than that?"

Over time I could see Abram change. He became less and less enthralled with the pantheon of gods Ur had to offer. Intellectually, he could not reconcile how anyone could worship a god they created from their own imagination. "How could anyone place their trust in a statue they carved out of wood?" He would ask.

Then one day he told me something astonishing. The God of the universe, the One Whom Noah served, spoke to him. "Abram," He said. "Leave your country, your family, and your father's house and go to a land I will show you. There I will make you a great nation. Those that bless you will be blessed by Me. Those that curse you will be cursed by Me. In you all the nations will be blessed."

A decision needed to be made. Did Abram trust Noah's God enough to leave the only place he called home? Could this God deliver what He promised? How would he become a great nation when he had no descendants? Why should he leave Ur, a place that he knew, to go to a place he didn't know? Oddly enough, as he was mulling over these questions, Noah's words kept ringing in his ear, "God offered me a life with Him. How could I value anything greater than that?"

The words haunted Abram. He shared with me his thoughts. "Here is a man that endured humiliation from everyone around him for one hundred twenty years while he built a mammoth vessel designed to save him and his family from a flood which had never occurred before in human history. But it did occur.

How did he deal with such a dilemma? He followed God. He walked with God. He trusted God. God spoke to him. Will He do the same for me?"

I told him that there was only one way to find out. My advice was sound, and he knew it. But going that route meant rejecting his father's practice and the way he had been taught all his life. In the final analysis he had the same option as did Noah. He could choose to believe that God is Who He claims to be, or He is not. That He will do what He says He will do, or He wouldn't. He is either capable of doing what He says, or He isn't. It is all a matter of faith. You either believe, or you don't. The concept was so simplistic, Abram thought it too good to be true.

Decisions are not always easy to make regardless of whether or not the desired outcomes are the right ones. Abram had a decision to make and only he could render a verdict. But I'll let him tell you all about it.

Chapter Six

Promises Made

Tradition can be a good thing or a bad thing depending on the perspective one has. In my case it was both positive and negative at the same time. On the positive side, I had godly men in the family lineage. Men like Noah. Even though I never met Noah, I heard story after story about him from Eber, who was himself a positive role model. These men had a steadfast faith in God. On the other hand, I was raised in a home where polytheism was taught and practiced. If it were not for the influence of Noah and Eber, I might never have heard about Elohim. Perhaps the best way to explain what I mean would be to start from the beginning.

Ur was the city of my birth. Natural resources were abundant so that permanent housing was common. There were few tent dwellers living in or near the general vicinity. Culturally, the city had an extensive library and spiritually, there was one of the largest ziggurats in existence, rivaled only by the one in Babylon.

My father, Terah, was one hundred thirty years old when I was born. I have two brothers, Haran and Nahor. Dad was seventy years old when Haran was born. Sarai was my wife. She was the daughter of my father, but not the daughter of my mother. At this point in our marriage Sarai has been unable to conceive a child. I have no heirs. I'm sure I don't need to tell you this, but my name is Abram.

That's enough background information for now. Let me share something that happened to me. As I alluded to earlier, I was raised in a polytheistic household. The patron god of Ur is Sin, the moon god. My father was a devotee of Sin. In the patriarchal system the father was the head of the family and everyone was expected to follow his lead. However, I heard these stories about Noah from Eber which raised questions in my mind. I just wasn't convinced by either side. Noah and Eber presented compelling reasons why there is one God, Elohim, and He was not willing to share His people with anyone. On the other hand, my family believed there were many paths to spirituality. One could follow one or more of the many gods in the pantheon. I struggled with those issues. One day when we lived in Ur, the God of Noah and Eber identified Himself and spoke to me. He said, "Leave your home, your family, and your father's house and go to a land that I will show you. I will make you a great nation. I will bless you and make your name great. Blessings will come to those who bless you and curses will come to those that curse you."

I was suddenly placed in a most awkward predicament. Who wouldn't want to be blessed? But on the other hand, I would have to leave everything and everyone with which and with whom I had become comfortable. I was caught off guard. He made it clear that He was the one looking for me and that He would put in place every circumstance to fulfill His promise of blessing. It was like a gift. I didn't do anything to deserve it. My only role in the whole endeavor was to accept or reject the offer.

Several things caused me immediate concern. First, how can I become a great nation, when my wife is barren? Second, He was asking me to leave my home and didn't tell me where I was going. Third, I would have to leave my extended family. All of these were genuine concerns. There were questions that needed answers. I felt like a fish in the river, being coaxed into the fisherman's net. The allure seemed positive, but what was in the net with which I was unaware? What is the negative?

My next step, if I were to accept the offer, was to begin the journey to wherever it was that Elohim wanted me to go. I said yes and informed my father of my decision. He was not pleased, but neither was he terribly upset. He would go with me. Before we could plan our getaway date, my brother Haran died. I had just celebrated my seventy-fifth birthday. Haran was one hundred and thirty-five years old when he died. After an appropriate funeral, Terah gathered us together and off we went in a northwest direction from Ur. In our party were Terah, myself, Sarai, and Lot, Haran's son.

We travelled northwest from Ur to the city of Haran, a trip of about seven hundred miles. Our route took us through Babylon. This wasn't a vacation. We were transporting all our possessions as well. It took us close to three months to complete the journey. Haran was an important city, but it paled in comparison to Ur. Nonetheless, the city offered an opportunity for us to increase our flocks which were already quite sizable.

I guess it was the combination of a strenuous trip and the death of my brother that contributed to my father taking a turn for the worse, health wise. He died shortly after we settled in Haran. His life spanned two hundred and five years. Both he and Haran died in the same year, two thousand eighty-three years after the creation.

Since I had already decided to follow the Lord's instructions, it was time to make a 100% commitment. With the move to Haran and the death of my father, there was no longer anything holding me back. Sarai and Lot joined me as we took the first step in our journey to follow Elohim. All our possessions were packed and placed on our donkeys. I knew the general vicinity in which to travel but Elohim did not tell me where in that general vicinity I should go. So, step by step I followed as He led me. Along the way, I wondered to myself, "Why me?" Elohim picked me to bless so I could be a blessing to others. I did nothing to deserve His attention and especially nothing to deserve to be blessed. As I struggled to ascertain the answer, I would occasionally ask someone for their advice. The answers I got back were not acceptable to me. One person said it was just a matter of being in the right place at the right time. Another person contended that it was merely a coincidence. One of my acquaintances from Ur said the stars were in the right alignment for me.

No, this was not random. It was no accident. I was handpicked. But why? Elohim picked me because He wanted to. He doesn't need a reason and He surely doesn't have to explain Himself to me. He chose me for a blessing, but He didn't force me to obey Him. He simply waited patiently for me to follow His lead.

We left Haran and travelled to Damascus, from Damascus to Hazor, Hazor to Megiddo, Megiddo to Shechem, and Shechem to Bethel a total of 515 miles. Upon arrival in Bethel, I constructed an altar to Elohim in appreciation for all He had done for us.

We settled in the hill country near Bethel. I pitched a tent for our shelter. This certainly wasn't like Ur. My setting in life was undergoing massive change. Physically, I was growing stronger, mentally, I was getting tougher, and spiritually, I was awakening, or so I thought.

Elohim spoke to me, saying, "To your descendants I will give this land." I still had no descendant much less descendants. So, I wasn't sure how this would work.

We had not been established in this new land very long when a famine struck. It took a toll on the family and my servants who came with me from Haran. As head of the family, it was up to me to provide. That task became harder and harder to accomplish. Some of the nomads that travelled through the area said there was plenty of food in Egypt. It seemed like the only responsible action was to take down the tent and travel to Egypt. I spoke to Sarai and Lot about it and made the decision to go. Unfortunately, I failed to speak to Elohim. I logically deduced, "After all, He gave me an intellect to reason and a will to decide. He expected me to use it." The truth of the matter is that it didn't even cross my mind to ask His opinion. My spiritual awakening was still in drowsy mode.

Making the trip to Egypt was not an easy task. There were tents to take down, people to consider, and livestock to be rounded up. Nevertheless, despite overwhelming odds, everyone in our family as well as our servants embarked on this journey. Starting from Hebron we travelled to Gaza and then on to the area of Memphis through the Nile delta. The trip was to cover three hundred miles. While we were on the way, Sarai and I had a serious conversation. I feared that the Egyptian men would find her so attractive that they would want her for themselves. If they thought she was my wife, they could easily kill me and had her for themselves. But if they thought she was my sister, there would be no need to kill me. I explained this to Sarai and asked her to tell anyone seeking information that she was my sister. After all, I rationalized, we had the same father. We just didn't have the same mother. It was at worst a half-truth. At the time I didn't quite grasp the notion that a half-truth is a whole lie. Nonetheless, Sarai agreed to the deception.

Our caravan arrived in Memphis. The Egyptian men did in fact appreciate Sarai's beauty. But their reaction was beyond what I had expected. They informed Pharaoh that a beautiful available woman was in his midst. As soon as Pharaoh heard about this woman, he sent for her and welcomed her into his harem. He gave me gifts of livestock as well as male and female servants. But Elohim protected Sarai from unwanted advances by sending plagues upon the Egyptians. Pharaoh knew I had something to do with the plagues. He called me to the palace and asked me why I would do such a thing. I explained my rationale to him, but to no avail. He was so upset that he ordered me out of his country. Sarai was returned to me. She was unharmed and spared from any affiliation with Pharaoh.

Upon returning to Israel, I knew that Lot and I needed to discuss a sensitive issue. We both had flocks when we arrived in Bethel. Now our flocks had increased and were interfering with each other. My experience with Pharaoh taught me a valuable lesson about asking Elohim for guidance in my decision-making process. So, I called on Him for wisdom. The Canaanites and Perizzites were living in the land, so it was important to set a good example for them in the decision that needed to be made, as well as how that decision was to be carried out.

The discussion started with both of us agreeing that our flocks were mingling with each other, causing some anxious moments between our herdsmen. If we continued in this direction, we would use up all the pasture land, adding more stress to an already touchy issue. The only logical solution was for the two clans to separate into two identifiable units. Lot would settle in one area and I would settle in another area. Lot was my nephew. In light of the death of both Terah and Haran, I was the patriarch and entitled to first choice where in the land to settle. But I abdicated that position and allowed Lot to choose in which direction he wanted to settle. Lot took a panoramic view of the land and chose the lushness of the Jordan Valley all the way to the southern-most tip of the Asphalt Sea. He journeyed southeast as far as Sodom before he pitched his tent.

Elohim spoke to me, saying, "Look both north and south, east and west. All the land you see I will give to you and to your descendants forever. They will be as numerous as the dust of the earth. Go! Walk over the land. It is yours. I will give it to you."

I did walk the land and settled in Hebron where I built an altar to Elohim.

One day as I was going about my daily routine, a male visitor arrived at my tent wanting to speak to Abram the Hebrew. The term Hebrew means "the man beyond the River" referring to the Euphrates River. That term was used to name Eber and associated with Abram. The man informed me that armies from the north had invaded the cities located at the southern end of the Asphalt Sea and had taken prisoners, of whom Lot was one. Lot was family. I had to take action. Three hundred eighteen of my trained men joined me in an effort to rescue the prisoners. The realization that we would be considerably outnumbered by this northern coalition did not enter our minds. We were on a mission, willing to die in order to save my nephew and those taken captive with him.

The coalition had the advantage, as they were significantly ahead of us on their way back to Shinar with the booty of war. We rode our animals hard for one hundred thirty miles in order to reach the captors. I spread the men out evenly around the enemy camp. Upon my command the men attacked from four different fronts. Even though we were outnumbered, the surprise attack worked. The enemy panicked, fleeing for their lives. We chased the deserters all the way to the north of Damascus where we overtook them and freed those they had taken captive.

The trip back to Canaan was interesting. The king of Sodom rode out to meet us. He offered to allow me to keep the booty as a reward for rescuing his people. I refused his offer. I told him I had taken a vow to El Elyon, God Most High that I would take nothing from him as a reward for this mission, lest he say to others that he made me rich. My only request was to give the men their due.

There was another interesting character who met us as well. His name was Melchizedek, king of Salem. As a priest of El Elyon, He blessed me, and I gave him a tithe.

After his rescue, Lot went back to Sodom. When he first moved there, he dwelt in a tent near Sodom. After a while he moved into the city, forsaking the life of a nomad. He became a permanent citizen living in a permanent structure.

Sarai and I had been in the land for several years, yet we had no children. The promise of me being a great nation seemed about as far off as it could possibly be. Elohim spoke to me in a vision saying, "Don't be afraid, Abram. You will have great reward." I responded, "What reward will you give me? I am childless and at this point my only heir is my servant Eliezer."

Elohim replied, "You shall have an heir your very own son. Look at the stars. Can you count them? Your heirs will be that numerous." As ludicrous as that sounded, I believed Him. That didn't keep me from wondering just how He was going to accomplish that feat. On that day Elohim made a covenant with me. He told me the boundaries of the land which He swore to give to me and my heirs. It was a large expanse of land from the Euphrates River on the east to the Nile River of Egypt.

When Sarai and I had been in the land for ten years, she came up with a plan. She would give me her handmaid, Hagar, given to her by Pharaoh when we were in Egypt, to be a surrogate. That would make me the legal father and Sarai the legal mother of the child to be born. I thought the idea was brilliant. God gave us intellect to think and will to act. We calculated an answer to the problem. Neither one of us thought to seek Elohim's opinion. We just made our own plans and carried them out.

I didn't think either Sarai nor Hagar considered the ramifications our plan would have on our psyche. I knew I didn't. The plan appealed to me in more than one way. It took a few months for Hagar to become pregnant. When that finally occurred, Hagar's attitude toward Sarai changed. She viewed her condescendingly. Sarai responded to Hagar's disrespect decisively. She demanded that I did something about the situation. She said, "Look what you have done. Hagar has treated me with derision. I have been wronged and you are to blame."

I replied, "This was your idea. How is it my fault? But rather than assessing blame, she is in your hands. Do what you want with her."

Sarai did just that. She treated Hagar so harshly that Hagar gathered her things together and ran away. She decided to go back where she came from, Egypt. She travelled in the direction of Shur, where she knew there would be water available. She stopped at the well. The Angel of the Lord spoke to her, "Hagar, Sarai's handmaid, where are you going and where have you come from?"

She responded, "My mistress, Sarai, has treated me harshly and I am running away."

The Angel of the Lord said to her, "Go back to Sarai and submit to her. You are pregnant with a son. You shall name him Ishmael, God hears, because I have heard your cries. Like an untamed donkey, He will be against everyone and everyone will be against him."

Hagar said, "You are El Roi, the God who sees. I have met Him who watches over me." She returned to Sarai and gave birth to a son. I named him Ishmael. Finally, I was a father at eighty-six years of age.

Thirteen years passed by. We celebrated my ninety ninth birthday. God appeared to me identifying Himself as El Shaddai, God Almighty. One thing I noticed about God was that He used different names to identify His various attributes. Elohim means strong one. He gave Hagar a sense of security and she called Him El Roi, the One Who Sees.

The Lord said, "Blamelessly walk before Me. We will enter into a covenant and I will multiply you profusely and will make you the Father of many nations. You will no longer be called

Abram. I give you a new name. From now on your name shall be Abraham, for I have made you the father of many nations. Kings will come from you. The covenant I will establish will be between you and Me and your descendants. It will be an everlasting covenant. As part of the covenant, I will give you and your descendants all the land that I promised as an everlasting possession. As a sign of the covenant, every male now living, and every male born hereafter shall be circumcised.

Your wife, Sarai, shall from this day forward be called Sarah. I will bless her, and she shall bear your son. You shall name him Isaac."

Both Sarah and I laughed when we heard what God had to say. How could a ninety-nine-year-old man and an eighty-nine-year-old woman produce a child? So, I said to God, "Ishmael shall live before you." But He answered back, "No! Sarah shall bear you a son this time next year and you will call him Isaac. I will establish my covenant with him." As for Ishmael, I have blessed him."

That very day all the males in the household were circumcised. I found that God has a sense of humor. The name Isaac means "laughter." Every time Sarah or I call his name we are reminded of El Shaddai. The God that established a covenant with me is all powerful. That gives me great comfort that despite what anyone has to say to the contrary, El Shaddai is willing and able to keep his word. He will do so not because my descendants and I am worthy of His fidelity. Rather, He will keep His word for His own names sake. He is a covenant keeping God.

Eber handed over the responsibility of family scribe to me. There is more to come about Isaac and my grandchildren.

Chapter Seven

The Promise Keeper

It was a typical day in Hebron, hot and humid. The terebinth trees outside our tent were providing just enough shade to lower the heat to a bearable level. Sarah was inside tending to her household duties, and I was sitting at the door of the tent, readying myself to check on the herdsmen, to offer whatever help they needed. Suddenly, three men appeared, walking toward the entrance of the tent. The one in the middle stood out from the other two. He had an aura about him.

I couldn't make out who they were, nor could I recall ever meeting any of the three. You can guess, to my surprise, when right then and there the one in the middle called me by the name given to me by El Shaddai. "Abraham!", he said as he tilted his head slightly to the left and nodded.

I responded, "Please sir, find me worthy to be in your company. Let me bring water to bathe your feet, provide a place of shade for you to rest, and prepare some food to sustain you as you travel onward." They replied in unison, "Let it be as you have said."

Hastily, I showed the three men to a place of shaded comfort where they could rest, went inside the tent to tell Sarah to bake some bread, selected a plump lamb from my flock, and instructed one of my servants to prepare a meal. Bites of cheese and a cup of cool milk were served as an appetizer.

After they had eaten, the conversation turned very personal. "Where is Sarah? they asked.

I answered, "In the tent."

The one in the middle said, "This time next year Sarah will deliver a son to you." From inside the tent, Sarah was listening. When she heard what he had to say, she thought to herself, "How humorous; are you telling me that this worn out woman, who is beyond child-bearing age is going to get pregnant?

"Why did Sarah laugh when I said next year at this time Sarah will deliver a son to you?" said the man. "Do you doubt that I can do as I say?

When He said this, I knew He was the Lord. I realized why He identified Himself as El Shaddai. What He was telling us would happen could only come-to-pass by the power of a being who is almighty. Not only could He cause a woman who is barren to have a child, He could also fulfill His promise of an everlasting covenant to me and my descendants.

After the meal was finished, the three visitors were planning on walking to Sodom, a distance of approximately thirty miles. As they started their trek, I heard the Lord say to the other two men, "I will not hide what I am about to do from Abraham." The other two men continued on their journey. The Lord told me that the people of Sodom were great sinners and He was going to destroy the city and everyone in it. I couldn't believe the Lord would destroy innocent people. I asked Him, "Lord will you destroy both the good and the bad? What if there were fifty righteous people in Sodom? Would You spare the city for the sake of those fifty? Will you do what is just?"

He replied, "If I find there are fifty righteous people in Sodom, I will spare the city for their sake."

I replied, "Lord, what if you only find forty-five people? Will you spare the city for those forty-five?"

Once again, He responded, "If there are forty-five righteous in the city, I will spare the judgment upon the city."

He and I continued on that line of conversation until I asked if there were ten righteous people would He spare the city. He said He would. I thought to myself, "Who do you think you are, trying to negotiate with God?

Having finished our conversation, the Lord went on His way and I returned to my tent.

Sleep evaded me that night. My level of anxiety was off the chart. Lot, my nephew, lived in Sodom and I worried for his safety. He came with me from Ur. We lived in the same proximity until our flocks became so large that we had to separate. I gave Lot first choice in deciding where to settle. He determined that the area of the Jordan Valley and land around the Asphalt Sea would best suit his needs. Despite the bad reputation of the people living in Sodom, he chose to pitch his tent near the city. Before long he moved into the city, and dwelt in a house with a solid foundation. He became so entrenched in the city over the past twenty years that he was considered a civic leader. Lot married a woman from the area and fathered two daughters.

The Lord revealed to me that the other two visitors that accompanied Him to my tent were angels. He disguised them as men, so they could be seen. When these two men entered Sodom, they found Lot sitting in the gate of the city in an official civic capacity. He was part of the welcome to Sodom committee.

The men arrived in Sodom just before dusk. Lot welcomed them and offered to house them at his home. He said, "Sirs, come to my house this evening where you can refresh yourselves, enjoy a good meal, and get a good night's sleep before you continue on your way."

The men responded, "That won't be necessary. We will spend the night in the town square."

Lot insisted they come to his house. They relented. Lot made them a feast, including fresh baked bread. After dinner, before they went to bed for the night, the men of Sodom surrounded Lot's house. They demanded that Lot bring the two men out to them, so they could satisfy their lust. Lot pled with the men of Sodom to reconsider their demands. He even offered to give them his two daughters instead of the two visitors. The men of Sodom would not be assuaged. Lot went outside to talk with them. They physically assaulted him. The two visitors struck the men of Sodom temporarily blinding them. They brought Lot safely inside the house.

The next morning the men informed Lot, his wife, and his two daughters that they would have to leave Sodom. Despite the danger experienced the night before, they were reluctant to leave. Finally, the two men took Lot and his family by their arms and pulled them out of the city, with the instructions not to look back. Lot's wife turned and longingly looked back at what she considered home. Instantly, she was turned into a pillar of salt.

After some discussion with the men, Lot and his two daughters went to the city of Zoar. When they were safely away from Sodom, God caused sulfur and fire to rain down on the city until it was destroyed.

Hebron was significantly higher in elevation than Sodom. Even though I was miles away from the city, I could see the smoke rising from the destruction. God remembered my entreaty to save the righteous and spared Lot from the judgment He brought on the city.

I sometimes wonder how I can escape a difficult situation and not learn from the circumstance. Sarah and I decided to move from our current location in Hebron to an area between Kadesh Barnea and the Wilderness of Shur, a distance of approximately fifty miles. On the way to our new location, I feared that the men of the area, where we were going to inhabit, would find Sarah beautiful and want her for their wife. So, I asked her to tell anyone who inquired that she was my sister. She agreed to the ruse. Sarah was ninety years old but still as beautiful as she was decades earlier. Gerar was one of the cities within the region we chose to inhabit. One day on a trip there, Abimelech, King of Gerar, saw Sarah and wanted her for his harem. When he asked the identity of this woman, we told him she was my sister. Abimelech took her just as we suspected. While Abimelech slept that night, he had a dream. The Lord appeared to him warning him of dire consequences as a result of taking another man's wife. Abimelech protested saying, "But they told me she was his sister."

"The Lord responded to him, "I know, and I did not allow you to touch her. Now, see to it that she gets back to her husband, and ask him to pray for you."

Abimelech arose from his slumber early the next morning and gathered his servants together to tell them what had transpired. He then called for me and asked why I would do such a thing. Looking for a good excuse, I told him it was out of fear that I tried to deceive him. Abimelech returned Sarah to me and gave me sheep, oxen, and servants both male and female. Then he told me to look at the land before me and choose wherever I wanted to make my home.

He turned to Sarah and said, "I have given Abraham silver coins to certify your innocence and vindicate you before anyone making false allegations."

As the Lord instructed, Abimelech asked that I pray for him and I did.

Sarah and I picked out a piece of land in the vicinity of Beersheba. We were still in Abimelech's territory. A disagreement arose about the usage of a well which belonged to me that was seized by one of Abimelech's men. I confronted Abimelech about it. We decided to enter into a treaty for everyone's benefit. As part of the treaty I gave Abimelech seven ewe lambs to demonstrate that there was no dispute that I dug the well. Once the treaty was enacted, Abimelech returned to his home and I planted a tree near the sight, and called on the name of the Lord, El Olam, The Everlasting God.

After thinking through this unfortunate circumstance, I took note of three things. First, how could I make the same mistake over again? While in Egypt during the famine twenty-four years ago, I was deported for being dishonest. It was a difficult lesson to learn. Yet, twenty plus years later, I was making the same mistake I made then. I could understand the thought entering my mind, but I couldn't comprehend falling for that trick again.

My reaction demonstrated how easy it was to allow personal fear to supersede right behavior.

Second, why didn't I ask Elohim for wisdom before I decided to move? Mistake number one was making an important decision without seeking God's will in the matter. Sarah and I made a decision to help God fulfill His promise to me of an heir. We put a plan in place without seeking God's direction. That didn't work out so well. What did I learn? That God doesn't need my help, but I need. His.

Third, why didn't I trust Elohim to protect me from those whom I perceived wanted to kill me?" Instead of trusting God as my protector, I relied on my own wiles to safeguard me from danger. El Elyon protected me when I went into battle to rescue Lot from the kings of the east. I reached out to Him and He became my shield. How was it that I so easily forget?

My actions confirmed in my heart that I am not now, or ever have been, or ever will be, deserving of the blessing that El Shaddai promised. I deserve His judgment, but He gives me what I don't deserve, and cannot earn - His love.

One year after El Shaddai spoke to me about an heir, Sarah delivered a baby boy. We named him Isaac just as we were instructed. His name means "he laughs," commemorating both Sarah's and my response to hearing the promise El Shaddai made to us. It was interesting that every time we called our son by his name that we were reminded of how nothing is impossible for El Shaddai. Every time our descendants spoke of Isaac, they would recall the faithfulness of El Shaddai. They would remember the promise and how that promise was fulfilled. They could take comfort in knowing that despite how their immediate circumstances might appear, El Shaddai was in control of those circumstances and how nothing is impossible with Him. When we received the promise, both Sarah and I had questions. The answer to our questions was El Shaddai. The answer to every question is El Shaddai. Knowing the facts, how could anyone not place their trust in Him and His promises?

Chapter Eight

Marriage: A Beginning, an Ending, and a Beginning Again

The last time I saw Eber he gave me the responsibility of being the family scribe. It was an important position, but not one that people clamored to chair. There was more to it than simply recording births and deaths. There was commentary involved as well. Explanations of behavior and significance of names were important facts to hand down. Let me give you an example.

One-way God revealed Himself to mankind is in His names. Thus far He has revealed His attributes to mankind in two basic names and several compound names. His basic names are Elohim and Adonai. Elohim means "Strong One" and "Adonai means

"Master." He had also revealed information about Himself in His compound names. El Shaddai means "God Almighty." He can do all things. El Roi means "The God Who Sees." Nothing escapes His sight. El Elyon means "God Most High." Man may serve other gods, but there is no god that can match Him. El Olam means "God Everlasting." He had no beginning and He will have no end. He is the eternal God.

It took all of these names and their meaning to bring me to the point of the story I am about to tell you. I might get emotional as I tell this story, so I am asking for your forgiveness in advance for my tears.

From the time, I was old enough to understand what being a father was all about, I wanted a son. I married early in life, and couldn't wait to start a family. Sarah, who was known as Sarai at the time, was barren. As hard as we tried and as badly as we wanted a child, our efforts were to no avail. The more that time went by, the more frustrating it became. When I was in my seventies an extraordinary event took place. The Lord visited me and made a promise that I would be a great nation. But I thought, how could that be when I had no descendants? Later He told me my descendants would be as numerous as the stars in the sky, but still no descendants. Finally, twenty-five years after making the first promise, El Shaddai caused Sarah's womb to be opened. Remarkably, at the age of ninety Sarah gave birth to Isaac.

Oh, how I love Isaac. The Lord Himself referred to Isaac as my only son. I loved Ishmael and wanted what was best for him, but Isaac was the one.

Ever since Sarah suggested that Hagar be her surrogate to provide an heir for me, there has been tension in the household.

Once it was bad enough that Hagar temporarily ran away. After Isaac was born, it got positively unbearable. I gave a feast celebrating Sarah weaning Isaac. Sarah noticed Ishmael laughing and assumed he was mocking Isaac. She was incensed and insisted that I drive both Hagar and Ishmael out of our community. I was reluctant to take such drastic action, but the Lord assured me that I should listen to Sarah. I did. That was all I wanted to say about that. T'was still a sore subject with me.

Time passed by. Isaac was an adolescent. Late one night, the Lord spoke to me. He said, "Take Isaac and offer him as a sacrifice to me." I could not believe what I just heard. This was Isaac, the son of promise. How could I possibly sacrifice him for any reason? Early the next morning, I arose and prepared to travel in the general direction to the place the Lord told me to go. Once again, the Lord would lead my steps to the exact spot where He wanted me to be.

Trust is a very personal issue. It means placing yourself in someone else's hands and believing they will act in your own best interest. You actually relinquish control of your life to someone or something other than yourself. In this particular situation, I was trusting the Lord to lead me to where I belonged. Step by step, I inched closer to Jerusalem. Lying in front of me was Mount Moriah. We had been traveling three days. The Lord called out to me, saying, "Here is the place. You and the boy climb to the summit of the mountain. There you will sacrifice the boy to me."

This entire episode seemed so surreal to me. My mind was reeling with questions and doubt. I wondered, "Did I hear God correctly? Why would He have me sacrifice Isaac? Did He not Himself say that Isaac was the son of promise? Does He plan on Sarah having another child?"

I was so caught up with my own thoughts that I wasn't paying attention to what Isaac or the servants were saying. Finally, they got my attention. I told the servants to stay where they were. Isaac and I would go up the mountain to sacrifice and then return to them. Isaac asked about the sacrifice. He was curious what we were going to offer. He saw that we had everything necessary for the offering except the sacrifice itself. I told him not to be concerned. The Lord would provide everything we needed.

When the two of us reached the place the Lord instructed me to go, I built the altar. Then came the conflict of faith. Do I blindly follow the instructions of the Lord, or do I follow my own gut instincts? That's when it finally dawned on me. I thought, "Why did God ask me to leave Ur and tell me to go to a land He would show me? Why did He save Sarah from being defiled by both Pharaoh and Abimelech? Why did He promise me an heir and wait twenty-five years to fulfill that promise? Why did He reveal Himself as the Strong One, the Master, the Most High, the All Powerful One, the All Seeing One, and the Everlasting God? He did all these things in order for me to believe that what He promises, He will fulfill. It is not necessary for me to understand how or why He will accomplish His will. It is only necessary for me to believe that He will.

With that in mind, I bound Isaac, placed him on the altar, and took my knife in hand to complete the sacrifice. As I placed the knife next to Isaac's carotid artery to slit his throat, the Angel of the Lord called out to me, "Abraham, stop what you are doing. Do not harm Isaac. You were willing to sacrifice him as you were commanded to do. Your trust in Me has proven authentic, even though you didn't understand why I asked you to sacrifice your son. You did not withhold from Me the one you loved most on the earth."

It was true. I did not know how God would do it, but I knew that He had the ability to create life, take life, and preserve life as He saw fit. That's why I told the servants that Isaac and I would return to them after we sacrificed on the mountain.

As I untied Isaac and helped him down from the altar, I noticed a ram caught by his horns in the thicket. I realized that God had provided the sacrifice just as I told Isaac He would. The ram was a substitute, sacrificed in Isaac's place. I named the place of sacrifice Jehovah Jireh, the Lord Will Provide.

The angel of the Lord spoke again. "I vow to bless you and multiply your descendants as numerous as the stars of heaven and the sand on the seashore, because you did not withhold your only son from Me. Since you obeyed My voice, all the nations of the earth will be blessed in you. All of the enemies of your descendants will be subservient to them."

Isaac and I rejoined the servants who had been waiting for us. Our entire party returned to Beersheba, where I decided to make my home for a season.

Sarah lived to be one hundred twenty-seven years old. Isaac was thirty-seven years old when Sarah passed away. I wanted to bury her near our dwelling in Hebron, so I approached Ephron the Hittite about purchasing the cave at Machpelah. He wanted to give me the property, but I insisted on paying for it. The price paid for the property was four hundred shekels of silver.

Before she died, Sarah and I talked about a wife for Isaac. Both of us agreed that it would not be good for Isaac to marry a Canaanite woman. My brother, Nahor, lived in Mesopotamia. I sent my oldest and most trusted servant to Mesopotamia to find a wife for Isaac. Upon his return, he shared the details of his trip. I think you will find them most interesting.

He began his story. "My name is Eliezer. Abraham, my master, trusted me with a most important task. He asked me to travel to Mesopotamia to find a wife for Isaac his son Now I know what you must be thinking. Isaac is nearly forty years of age. Surely, he is capable of finding his own wife. But our tradition is for marriages to be arranged by the patriarch of the family.

As I travelled, I marveled at the importance my master placed on the success of the venture. He insisted I take a solemn oath to follow his instructions to the letter.

The distance between Hebron and Mesopotamia is approximately five hundred miles. Normally, it would take a month to make that trip, but I was on a mission from my master. It only took me twenty-two days to make the trip.

Just outside of the town where Nahor lived, was a spring, that supplied the water for the residents of the community. It was common practice for the women of the village to come at sunset to draw water from the well. I asked the God of my master Abraham for a sign to allow me to discern which young woman He wanted me to approach as a wife for Isaac. The sign would be the young woman's response to my request for a drink of water from the well. When I asked for a drink, the woman would respond, 'While you drink, I will water your camels.' This will be my assurance that this is the young woman you have selected as a wife for Isaac.

"While I was still praying, a young woman by the name of Rebekah came to the well. She was the daughter of Bethuel, who was the son of Milcah, the wife of Nahor, Abraham's brother. I watched as she went to the well, dipped her water jug into the well, and extracted the night's supply of water. As she departed from the well, I asked her for a drink. She responded, 'While you drink and refresh yourself, I will draw water for your camels.'"

"I was astounded at the young woman's response.'" But even more so, I was completely taken aback by how this drama was unfolding.

"After the camels were watered, I took jewelry I brought with me and gave it to the young woman. There was a gold ring and two bracelets. I asked her, '"Is there room in your father's house for overnight guests?"'

"She responded, "There is plenty of room in my father's house for you and ample stable room for your camels." I was overwhelmed with emotion. I had just been a part of, and a witness to, a miracle. The God of my master, Abraham, provided a wife for the son of promise.

"I explained the scenario to Bethuel, how God answered my prayer and led me too Rebekah. I told him that I would be leaving in the morning to return to Hebron and requested permission to take Rebekah with me. Bethuel recognized God's hand in all of these circumstances and granted permission to take Rebekah as the Lord directed. I gave gifts of garments, jewelry, and costly ornaments to Bethuel, her brother, Laban, and the young woman's mother.

The next morning as we prepared to leave, Laban and the young woman's mother requested we wait ten days before we leave. I explained to them how the Lord's hand was clearly in this situation and requested their permission for immediate departure. They were reluctant to comply and suggested that Rebekah be consulted as to whether she wanted to go with me.

Rebekah did not hesitate to answer. She replied, '"I will go with him."'

Rebekah, and her nurse, Deborah, joined our entourage as we embarked on the return trip to Hebron. The pace of travel was not as brisk returning to Hebron as it was in going to Mesopotamia. We stayed on The King's Highway all the way to the south of the Asphalt Sea. This southern route took us through the eastern part of the Negev. We passed through Zoar heading northwest toward Beersheba. We were travelling in the arid region of the country when we saw someone in the distance. When Rebekah saw the man, she dismounted her camel, and wanted to know who this man was. I immediately recognized him as Isaac. When I revealed the identity of the man, Rebekah placed her veil over her face, in keeping with the tradition of the bride veiling her face until the wedding ceremony.

I went to Isaac and explained everything to him in detail, so that he would get a full understanding of how the Lord worked all things for His glory. He escorted Rebekah to the tent that Sarah occupied until her death. Isaac took Rebekah as his wife.

All of us were in a celebratory mood. We had successfully traversed a difficult terrain, witnessed a memorable wedding, and experienced the comfort God provides when you trust in Him."'

Finding a wife for Isaac relieved a great deal of stress for me. As tenaciously I hold on to the reality of God's sovereignty, His ability to do the impossible, and His vow to keep His promises, I must admit that doubt still creeps into my mind. The issue is not whether God will keep His word. He will always do that! The issue is not whether God is capable of the impossible. He is! The issue is not whether God has an equal. He doesn't! These are facts. These are what my mind knows as truth. These are the facts that led me to take Isaac to Mount Moriah to sacrifice him to the Lord. I believed God would deliver him. But there is another component that dwells within my mind. God created me with intellect, the ability to think, emotion, the ability to feel, and will, the ability to choose. Theoretically, facts should always outweigh feelings. However, my ability to feel sometimes overrides my ability to think and I choose the wrong course of action. That doesn't mean I have lost faith or no longer believe. It simply means I am a human being, wanting to do what is right but unsure what the right thing is. Flawed and frail, I struggle with the right course of action, allowing stress to have an unhealthy effect on my life.

Sarah was the love of my life. Her death prompted me to consider my mortality. There were important matters I felt needed immediate attention. That's why I made Eliezer swear to me he would follow my directions to find a wife for Isaac. You will recall that earlier we talked about Isaac being forty years old when he married Rebekah. Part of that was my fault. It was my responsibility to arrange a marriage for Isaac. It was an important matter, but one which I thought there was plenty of time to accomplish. I procrastinated. When Sarah died, I theorized that time was of the essence. I could not rest until Eliezer reported back to me that his mission was a success.

Three years had gone by. My grief for Sarah had subsided and the pressure of Isaac's wife was remedied. I remarried. Keturah was her name. Prior to our marriage, I bequeathed all I had to Isaac. Keturah and I had six sons. I gave each of them gifts and sent them away from Canaan to live in the east. This way there would never be a question as to the rightful heir.

Isaac and Rebekah learned early in their marriage that Rebekah was barren. Just like Sarah and me, the couple yearned to have children, but none would occur. Isaac petitioned the Lord and He opened Rebekah's womb and she conceived twins. She knew the boys were going to present a challenge. They struggled mightily in her womb prompting her to ask the Lord what was wrong. He replied, "Two clans are in your womb, one is stronger than the other with the older one serving the younger one."

When it was time for her to deliver, the boys practically came out together. The first born was red in appearance, with the second holding on to the first's heel. Esau was the firstborn and Jacob was next. The boys were as different as they could be. Esau was the alpha male. He was confident, direct, and the word failure was not in his vocabulary. Jacob, on the other hand, was secretive, emotional, and sensitive. Esau was a hunter while Jacob was more of a homebody. Isaac was partial to Esau while Rebekah was partial toward Jacob.

Knowing that my time was getting short, I gave the family scribal responsibilities to Isaac. I was one hundred sixty years old at the time. There is more to be learned regarding Isaac and his two boys. Isaac will be happy to fill you in on the details.

Chapter Nine

Isaac and the Challenge of Twin Boys

Having twin boys is a real challenge, especially when there is so much competition for attention among them. Admittedly, Rebekah and I made a mistake when we showed favoritism to one boy over the other. That is the case involving Esau and Jacob. I liked the manly qualities that Esau presented, and Rebekah liked the sensitive side of Jacob's personality. It wasn't as though we loved the one and hated the other. We loved them both, just not equally.

Esau would go on hunting expeditions and bring back his quarry to make a savory stew. Jacob was more of a thinker than a doer. Esau didn't regard tradition as much as Jacob. Let me give you an example.

One-day Esau went on one of his hunting trips. He was gone all day, stalking his prey. He dragged his catch back and prepared it for preservation. By this time, he was exhausted. Meanwhile, Jacob had prepared a meal of his own. The aroma of the simmering stew was so intoxicating to Esau that he was willing to trade his birthright for a hearty bowl of the boiling fare. He asked Jacob for a bowl of the stew. Jacob was more than happy to accommodate the request under certain conditions. Knowing that Esau did not value tradition, Jacob, whose name means "he seizes," was willing to barter a bowl of stew for Esau's birthright. All Esau wanted was a bowl of stew. He didn't think anything beyond that. He agreed to the conditions and gave up his birthright.

At about the same time, my father died. He was one hundred seventy-five years old. He led an eventful life and was known as the 'Friend of God.' Ishmael, my half-brother, and I buried Abraham in the cave of Machpelah, which he purchased from Ephron the Hittite, to bury my mother. Ishmael was eighty-nine years old. He was the father of twelve princes of the Arab world. They settled from the Wilderness of Shur to the northern part of Arabia. The six sons of Keturah were also half-brothers who resided in eastern Arabia. Add my two sons, Ishmael, and me, made a total of twenty-two descendants of Abraham when he died. Just as the Lord promised, Abraham was the father of many nations.

I was seventy-five years old when I buried my father. I couldn't help but remember the stories my father and mother told me about how difficult it was waiting for a child. When the promise from God didn't seem to materialize, they thought of a plan to help the situation along, only to be disappointed in the outcome. Finally, after all hope was lost, the Lord delivered on His promise in the most extraordinary way. That is the lesson I take from all of us being together for the burial. When your hopes seem as though they will never be fulfilled, look for God to act in a way that only He can act. My father left a legacy of faith for all to follow. He was not a perfect man, but he had a 'Friend' in high places.

There was a famine in the land and I wanted to be proactive in dealing with this dilemma. I was on my way to Gerar to see Abimelech. The Lord spoke to me saying, 'Stay in this land and do not go to Egypt. I am with you and will bestow my blessing on you and your offspring. I will fulfill my promise to Abraham to give you and your descendants the land I promised.'"

So, I made my home temporarily in Gerar. Rebekah was a beautiful woman. When the men of Gerar began to ask questions about her, I told them she was my sister, for fear they would want to do me harm. We had been living in the community for some time, when Abimelech saw me acting toward Rebekah more like a husband than a brother. Abimelech confronted me. saying, 'This woman is not your sister, is she? She is your wife. What are you trying to do to us?

"I quickly replied, 'I feared you or the men in the community would find her attractive, and kill me if anyone thought she was my wife.'

Abimelech said, "If any man had been intimate with her, great guilt would have been suffered by all of us." He issued a decree saying, "Anyone touching Isaac, or his wife will be put to death."

We stayed in the area, sowed, and reaped the land for a great harvest. The Lord blessed us by increasing our flocks and herds.

We also had to increase the number of workers we employed. Much to the chagrin of the other residents, we were thriving in the face of the famine. Our success and their jealousy made for poor neighbors. Finally, Abimelech asked us to leave the area.

I had lied, disrespected Rebekah, and placed the residents of Gerar in jeopardy. As undeserving and unworthy as I was, the Lord kept His word and still blessed me.

We left the immediate area and settled in the valley. It wasn't long before another dispute began to brew. My herdsmen and the herdsman of Gerar became embroiled in a controversy over rights to the wells in the valley. I insisted the wells were dug by Abraham and rightfully belonged to him. The men of Gerar maintained they were the rightful owners. Abimelech and I resolved the issue and entered into an agreement that neither party would seek to harm the other. A feast celebrating the agreement was held before Abimelech and his men departed. Shortly thereafter, my servants brought news that they had found an adequate water supply.

Esau was somewhat of a maverick. He certainly wasn't a conformist. Tradition, standards, or community norms meant little to him. I must admit, there was something about his rebelliousness that I admired. Rebekah, on the other hand, was not so accommodating. She found his dissident attitude to be unappealing. She was especially irritated when, at the age of forty, he married two Hittite women. Knowing full well the lengths that his grandfather went to find a suitable wife for me, his outright rejection of that process was offensive.

When I was one hundred thirty-seven years old, legally blind, and feeling I was reaching the end of my life, I beckoned Esau to come to me. "Please, go out into the wilderness and catch me some wild game. Then, if you don't mind, make me my favorite meal."

We always had a good, open relationship, so it came as no surprise that he gathered together his bow, a quiver full of arrows, and a knife in preparation for the hunt. I told him, "Upon your return, I will bless you."

Rebekah heard everything that was said. She summoned Jacob to her tent and instructed him to pick out from the flock two goats that she might prepare one of Isaac's favorite meals. She told Jacob, "After he has eaten, he will give you the blessing."

Jacob hesitated to go. "What if he questions me? What if he asks me to draw near? If he touches me, he will immediately know I am not Esau. Esau is a hairy man, while my skin is smooth. If he suspects it is me, he might curse me instead of giving me his blessing." Rebekah convinced Jacob to go along with the plan.

"I may have had diminished eye sight, but my hearing and feeling senses were in good working order."

Rebekah took some of Esau's clothing and put them on Jacob so that he smelled like him. Then she sewed the skins Jacob had peeled from the two goats and made a covering with them. Placing the skins on Jacob, she said, "Now Isaac will feel the skins and know that it is Esau."

Jacob was not too keen on the idea, but he came to me to serve the food I had requested. I was suspect. My first reaction was, "Who are you?' Jacob anticipated my response'

He replied, 'It's Esau. I have done what you asked. Try some of the food I brought you.'

"How did you catch the game and prepare the food so quickly,' I asked.

"The Lord granted me speed in completing your charge to me,' Jacob replied.

Come closer so I can feel you to convince myself that you really are Esau.' I countered.

Jacob moved close enough for me to touch him. 'I am a little confused,' I cried. "The voice that is speaking to me is Jacob, but the skin is Esau. Are you really Esau." I asked.

"Bring me the food you prepared.' I said.

As he stood next to me, I could smell his clothing. It was definitely the smell of Esau. We kissed each other on the cheek and I gave Jacob the family blessing. The entire ordeal was stressful.

Jacob barely had time to leave my tent when Esau returned from the hunting trip. He brought the meal he had prepared for me. When Esau announced his presence, I knew I had been deceived. "Who are you?" I cried out.

"I am Esau, your son. I hunted game and prepared a meal for you as you requested."

"If you are Esau, who was it that prepared the food I just ate, and received the blessing I just gave?" I asked in hushed tones.

Esau began to weep. Through his tears he cried out, 'Do you not have a blessing for me? Jacob took my birthright and now he takes the blessing that was clearly mine. O father, is there nothing left for me?'

By this time, I too was sobbing. It was a heartbreaking moment. I told Esau, 'Your brother deceived me, and I gave him the blessing that was yours. I made you his servant and blessed him with abundance of sustenance. As for you, my son, regrettably, you will dwell away from prosperity in arid places. You shall live by the sword, serving your brother. Restlessness will be your companion until the yoke is broken from your neck."

Esau was devastated. He hated Jacob and wanted to kill him. He thought, "When my father dies, I will exact revenge on Jacob for what he has done."

Rebekah knew her sons and anticipated Esau's retaliation. It wasn't long before she received word that Esau planned to kill Jacob. She called Jacob to her tent to warn him of his brother's plan to kill him. She further instructed him to flee to the land of her brother, Laban, where he could take refuge from Esau, cautioning him to stay there until she informed him it was safe to return.

Rebekah spoke to me about the matter. She reminded me that Esau had married two Hittite women against her wishes and how adamant she was about Jacob not doing the same. I called Jacob to my tent. It was an awkward meeting, in light of the conspiracy to deceive, in which Rebekah and Jacob had been complicit. Nonetheless, I warned Jacob about marrying a Canaanite woman, and encouraged him to take a wife from Rebekah's relatives in Paddan-aram. Then I prayed over him that God would grant him the promises made to Abraham; which He had confirmed to me. Promises of a land and descendants as numerous as the stars of the sky. Jacob was seventy-seven years of age when he left.

I also passed on to him the responsibility of being the family scribe. After all I was one hundred thirty-seven years old at that time. It was time for someone else to take over and I knew this task would not be easy, nor would it fit Esau's strengths. Jacob was the only viable choice.

Esau was livid when he learned that Jacob was on his way to Paddan-aram. His opportunity for revenge was temporarily placed on hold. That wasn't bad enough. He also knew that I had given him instructions that he was not to take a wife from the Canaanites. For Esau that was a further slap in the face. He had two wives and both of them were Canaanites. He might have understood had they been newlyweds, but he had been married to them for thirty-seven years. He questioned, "Have my wives done anything to reflect badly on themselves during the past thirty-seven years?" To further exacerbate the situation, Esau went to Arabia and married one of Ishmael's daughters. My mother, Sarah, would have rolled over in her grave had she known that her grandson married a daughter of Ishmael.

I don't know how much time I have left on this earth, but the time I have had has been interesting.

Chapter Ten

Things Are Not Always The Way They Seem

When you start out in life with a name that means "he deceives" you are operating from a disadvantage. I am Jacob and that is what my name means. There are three stories circulating about me that portray me as the bad guy. You have heard one side of the story, but I would like you to hear it from my perspective.

As you know, Esau and I were twins. He was the firstborn and I came along just moments later. We gave our mother, Rebekah, fits both in and out of the womb. Rebekah favored me and Isaac, my father, favored Esau. We were constantly competing with one another.

Esau was a gifted hunter. He would often go into the wilderness and come home with game for Rebekah to cook for dinner. Both Esau and I were capable cooks as well. Once when Esau went on a hunting expedition, I cooked a pot of lintel stew. The stew was simmering in the cauldron when Esau returned from a long day of hunting. He was famished and requested a bowl of the stew. I knew that his birthright meant very little to him. So, when he asked for a bowl of stew, I bartered with him; a bowl of stew for a birthright. I thought that was a fair deal. He got what he wanted, and I got what I wanted. After all, our births were so close together. But whenever the episode is mentioned, I am the villain. It is as though I stole something from him, rather than Esau giving something away of his own accord.

The second example is the day I obtained the blessing that Isaac was going to give to Esau. Notice, I didn't say he was due the blessing. Remember, I held the birthright. Esau voluntarily gave it up. Isaac favored Esau and wanted him to have the blessing. He was proactive in his zeal to bless Esau. He knew full well that Rebekah would have nothing to do with that idea had she been aware of what he was up to. When she learned about Isaac's misguided notion, she summonsed me and devised a plan to supersede Isaac's. It wasn't my idea. I balked at her first suggestion. She commanded me to deceive my father. Could I have said no? Of course. But why would I, knowing that my father was acting contrary to the tradition of the birthright.

Consider also the fact that Esau married two Canaanite women, unlike the practice that Abraham established about not allowing Isaac to marry a Canaanite woman.

Finally, there was the prophecy about the older serving the younger. When we were struggling with each other in the womb, and Rebekah asked the Lord what was going on. He told her the older, that would-be Esau, would serve the younger, that would-be me. All of these factors should be considered before rendering a judgment. Isaac knew about these circumstances, yet proceeded to make plans to give the blessing to Esau.

I hope you can see that everything is not as cut and dry as people have been assuming. There are extenuating circumstances that must be taken into consideration, that constitute the other side of the story.

We will address the third incident a little later.

After the blessing fiasco, at the suggestion of both Isaac and Rebekah, I left for Paddan-aram. Esau was plotting to kill me, and I was wifeless. Isaac was one hundred thirty-seven years old and thought he was near the end of his life. Little did he know that he would live another forty-three years. Before I departed, Isaac gave me the responsibility of the family scribe.

Paddan-aram was the home of Rebekah's brother Laban. It was an area situated in the vicinity of the Euphrates River. Haran was located within the area of Paddan-aram. Haran was the city where Abraham lived until the death of his father, Terah. I would be safe there and it gave me opportunities to find a wife. It might surprise you to know that I was seventy-seven years old at the time. Rather late in life to be looking for a wife.

The total distance to travel from Beersheba to Haran was approximately five hundred miles. Three days into my travel, I stopped near the village of Luz, some people refer to the town as Bethel. The sun had already set. I was wearied from a long day's travel. I unpacked my bedroll on the softest place I could find, selected a rock for a pillow, and made myself as comfortable as possible. It didn't take long before I was sound asleep. I dreamed I saw a ladder spanning from heaven to earth. Angels were climbing up and down the ladder. At the top of the ladder stood the Lord. He spoke, "I am the Lord, the God of Abraham and Isaac. I will give to you and your descendants the land upon which you sleep. Your descendants will be innumerable, as the dust of the earth. I am with you, will not leave you, and will return you to this land."

When I awoke, I realized how blessed I was and what a special place I was occupying. I took the stone that I used for a pillow, erected a pillar on that site, and poured oil on it, commemorating the time and place where the Lord revealed Himself to me. I took a vow that day, saying 'If God will grant me perseverance, provide food to eat, and clothes to wear, so that I can come again to my father's house, then the Lord shall be my God. I will give a tithe to the Lord.

Following that ceremony, I set out once again for Paddan-aram. My destination was still more than four hundred fifty miles and twenty-three days away.

Outside the village of Haran, there was a well, where I stopped to refresh myself and the animals. It was watering time for the flocks in the area. The well was protected by a large round stone. There were three flocks of sheep gathered there. The shepherds were waiting for the other flocks to arrive before they moved the stone.

I called out to them, 'Men, where do you live?'

They responded, 'We live in Haran.'

I asked them if they knew Laban, the son of Nahor?'

'We do know Laban!' they responded.

'How is he?' I asked.

'He is well. Look there is his daughter, Rachel, coming with the sheep.'

"Why don't you water your sheep and take them to pasture? Jacob asked.

'It's too early. We must wait until all the flocks are present, then we will remove the stone and water the sheep,' they replied.

By this time Rachel had arrived with her sheep. I approached the well, removed the stone, and watered the sheep Rachel brought with her. I then kissed Rachel, telling her I was Rebekah's son. Rachel ran to tell her father that one of their kinsmen was at the well.

Laban did not tarry but ran with haste to see me. We embraced and greeted each other with a kiss. Laban invited me to come to his house, saying 'You are surely my flesh and bones. Stay here with me.'

A month passed by. Laban spoke to me, saying 'We are relatives. You have been working alongside us since your stay here began. You haven't expressed any concern toward being compensated for your work. What shall we establish your wages to be?'

Laban had two marriageable age daughters, Rachel and Leah. Leah was the older of the two. Rachel was beautiful, and I fell in love with her. I answered Laban. "I will work for you seven years, if you will give me Rachel for my wife."

Laban responded, "I would rather give her to you than any other man. Stay with me."

I stayed with Laban for seven years. At the end of that period, I said to him, "The time of our agreement is complete. Now, give me Rachel as my wife." Laban wanted to celebrate the occasion by having a marriage feast. He invited his friends and neighbors to gather for a great party.

That night, after the sun had gone down, Rachel and I were to have our own tent where we could privately consummate our marriage. Laban instructed me to wait in the tent while he escorted the bride to her bridal chambers. Finally, after seven years Rachel and I would be husband and wife.

When I awoke, the morning sun was peeking through the opening in the tent. My bride was lying next to me. But much to my shock, it wasn't Rachel. It was Leah. I bolted out of bed and rushed to Laban, asking "What have you done to me?"

Laban responded, "Our tradition calls for the older to be married before the younger. Leah is the older. Complete the week of celebration, and I will give you Rachel as well, if you agree to work for me another seven years."

I agreed to his conditions and finished the week. Laban was true to his word and gave Rachel to me as my wife. Life was somewhat awkward having two wives; especially since I loved Rachel. Laban gave servants to both women. He gave Zilpah to Leah and Bilhah to Rachel.

Leah was in a difficult situation. The Lord had mercy on her and opened her womb. But Rachel remained barren. Leah bore four sons to me, Reuben, Simeon, Levi, and Judah. She was hopeful with each birth that we would develop a loving relationship. But it wasn't to be.

Rachel wanted desperately to have children, but she could not. She decided to have Bilhah act as her surrogate and bear children to me. Bilhah conceived and bore two sons to me, Dan and Naphtali.

Leah made her servant Zilpah her surrogate. Zilpah conceived and bore two sons, Gad and Asher.

Leah and Rachel were in a contest to win my love. They felt that the more children they gave to me the greater would be my love for them.

Rachel was still barren, but Leah bore two more sons, Issachar and Zebulon. She also bore a daughter named Dinah.

Finally, the Lord opened Rachel's womb and she bore a son, Joseph. I went to Laban, informing him that I wanted to go back to my own country. He was persuasive in convincing me to stay. He knew the Lord had blessed him through the work of my hands. He did not want to give me up. I offered a solution to the problem. I told Laban that I would stay if he allowed me to go into his flocks and pick out all the speckled and spotted sheep, and black lamb. They shall be my wages. Laban agreed to the request. However, before I could take the animals, Laban sent his men to remove all the striped and spotted male goats and all the speckled and spotted female goats. I was left with white sheep, both male and female, brown females, and speckled males. Laban established a place for me to take my family, a village approximately fifty miles away.

Animal husbandry is my specialty. I know the elementary aspects of breeding sheep. I took sticks from poplar, almond, and plane trees and whittled them until the fragrance inside could be smelled by the sheep. The odor is similar to the scent given off when an animal is in heat. The sheep would mate, and I would separate the offspring into the various categories. Laban's sheep would be placed in his sheepfold, and the speckled and spotted would be placed in my sheepfold. The increase to my sheepfold was rapid.

This is where the third story about me, that I mentioned earlier, began to circulate. The facts are that Laban had deceived me over seven years earlier about marrying Rachel. I worked for him seven years when I was supposed to marry Rachel. Instead, he substituted Leah without my knowledge or consent. After a week of marriage celebration, he gave me Rachel on the condition I work for him another seven years. I did that. Then when I wanted to return to my land, he wanted me to stay and continue working for him. It was time for me to work for myself and not be oppressed by someone else. I did not steal or mislead. I simply used my knowledge of mating sheep along with the help of God to increase and protect my assets just as anyone else would do.

Laban was not happy with me. He knew that I had outsmarted him, and he no longer looked on me the same way he had in the past. His sons claimed that I gathered my wealth by taking what belonged to their father, and by extension to them. It seemed to me that conditions were rapidly deteriorating into a hostile situation. The Lord saw all the tricks Laban had played on me. He said, "Return to your homeland and I will be with you."

I went to the tents of Rachel and Leah to explain the situation. They responded, "There is nothing to keep us here. We have been treated as foreigners. If God has told you to leave this area, then we must go."

My men and I gathered together all our belongings, placed my wives and children on camels, and set out for Beersheba.

It took Laban three days to learn that we were fleeing Paddan-aram for Beersheba. He began his pursuit, and pushed hard to overtake us, finally reaching us in the mountains of Gilead. God warned Laban in a dream to carefully consider his options in dealing with me.

Laban appeared more hurt than angry. He asked, "Why did you steal away into the night, carrying off my daughters, as if they were captives? You didn't allow me to bid my daughters and grandchildren farewell. I could have thrown a going away party for them. Why did you steal my gods?"

Jacob answered, "Your attitude and the attitude of your sons has changed dramatically toward me. Both you and Your sons think I stole from you. I was worried you would do me harm. I am unaware of your missing gods."

A thorough search was conducted to locate Laban's gods. Anyone found hoarding these gods would be subject to serious repercussions. I learned later that Rachel had taken the gods and hid them from everyone's sight. Both of us had our say about each other. Finally, after the tension eased, a proposal was made that we enter into a covenant not to seek the other for harm. Early the next morning Laban and his men departed and returned to Paddan-aram.

The encounter with Laban was extremely stressful. Emotions had been at fever pitch for months. As I proceeded to my destination, angels from God met me. Just when I needed encouragement, God sent His messengers to cheer me up. He knew what my next encounter was going to entail. I didn't.

It was time to make amends with Esau. Our route took us directly through Edom, the home place for Esau. I sent messengers informing him, I had spent the past twenty years with Laban, accumulating assets. Now, I am returning home, to serve out my years with our father. As a token of peace, I am sending my messenger ahead with gifts of sheep, livestock, and camels. I want to make things right between us."

That night I had a most unusual experience. All night there was a man wrestling with me. I held onto the man wanting to know his identity. Finally, at daybreak, the man touched my hip causing me great pain. But I held onto him making sure he understood I would not let go until he blessed me.

He asked, "What is your name?"

"I told him Jacob," to which he replied, "From now on you will be known as Israel."

I asked for his name. He replied, "Why do you ask for my name?"

I answered him, "I have wrestled with God and have seen Him face to face and lived."

One of the servants called my attention to a group of men approaching on horseback. Even though they were far away, I recognized Esau leading the group. Not knowing what to expect, I placed the servants and their children up front, followed by Leah and her children, with Rachel and Joseph last. Then I took my place in the front of the line. Bowing as I walked seven times, I came near to my brother.

Esau dismounted and ran toward me. At first, I was alarmed, but that anxiety disappeared as Esau wrapped his arms around me, kissed my neck, and began to weep. I, too, wept for joy as the two of us were reconciled. Esau spoke first. "Who are these with you?" He asked.

"These are my servants and their families, followed by my wives and children that God has blessed me with," I replied.

What was the purpose for all the animals your messengers brought to me?" Esau inquired.

"I sent gifts to curry your favor, "I replied.

"That isn't necessary. I have plenty," He said.

"Please accept my gifts. God has been gracious to me with what I have and now He has restored you to me," I urged him.

"Very well!' he replied. 'I will go ahead of you to ensure your safety.'

"That won't be necessary. We will see each other in Seir," I said. However, we did not make it to Seir. Instead, we went to Succoth and then on to Shechem. This fulfilled the promise God made to me over twenty years ago, when He said "He would indeed bring me back safely." I called Him El Elohe Israel, the Mighty One of Israel.

God instructed me to leave Shechem and go to Bethel. As we travelled, God caused a great fear to come over the people of the land. As a result, my enemies did not pursue me. I was to make an altar there to God, Who answers me in the day of my distress and, Who has been with me wherever I have gone. While in Bethel, God again said, "You are no longer to be called Jacob. From now on you will be called Israel. I am El Shaddai. A great nation shall come from you. Kings will come from your own body. The promise I made to Abraham and Isaac, I confirm with you. I give this land to your descendants."

Rachel and I had another son. His name is Benjamin. My beloved Rachel died delivering him. I buried her in Bethlehem. Sometime afterward, I went to Hebron where Isaac lived. I was able to spend some time with him before he died. He was one hundred eighty years of age. Esau and I buried him.

My son, Joseph, was always special to me. I haven't mentioned him very much because I wanted him to tell his own story. That is the reason I made him the family scribe. He will tell you more about what happened after the death of Isaac.

Chapter Eleven

Joseph

Jacob had twelve sons. I was the eleventh but the first one born to Rachel. Jacob was ninety-one years old when I was born. He and Rachel had an abiding love for one another. That may explain why he was so partial to me, and why he chose me for the role of family scribe.

There is not much to tell about the first seventeen years of my life, but there are two events that stand out. The first is an ongoing event. It is the partiality with which Jacob indulged. I was alienated by my brothers through no fault of my own. They grew weary of seeing me receive kudos for nearly everything I did, whether I deserved it or not. The words, "Why can't you be more like Joseph," were not uttered, but the sentiment sure was a reality. At one point, Jacob gave me an extremely nice multi-coloured outer garment. It was the sort of garment a king would give to the prince in anticipation of him one day assuming the throne. To my brothers it was a reminder that I had already been preselected to rule over the family.

The second event centered on two dreams that I had. In the first dream, the boys were out in the field. The older boys were reaping the stalks of grain with the scythe. The younger boys were gathering the grain that had been cut and bundling them together in sheaves. Without notice, each boy's sheaves came alive. My sheaf stood upright, and the sheaves of my brothers bowed down to my sheaf. In my naivete, I shared the dream with my brothers. It wasn't my intent to further alienate myself from them, but that is exactly what happened. They reacted strongly to the dream. They practically shouted, "Do you think we are going to bow down to you? You will not rule over us despite what Jacob might think." They hated me even more.

The second dream included Jacob and Rachel as well as the boys. In this dream, the sun, moon, and eleven stars were bowing down to me. The boys said, "Here you go again, trying to establish superiority over us. We are tired of your dreams and your condescending attitude."

When I told Jacob the dream, he reacted negatively as well. He said, "Do you think your mother, brothers, and I will bow down to you? Who do you think you are?"

I should have anticipated my brother's reaction. They were jealous of my relationship with Jacob and resented me for it. But Jacob's reaction caught me off guard. His rebuke cut me to the very core.

That was a picture of my everyday life. If people were given the option of commenting on why I shared those dreams with my brothers, the views would look something like this:

"What a snob. His brothers were right about him."

"Spoiled brat."

"His way of getting even with his brothers."

"What was he thinking?"

That may be the way it seems, but that was not my thought process. I did not sit down and try to come up with a way to get even with my brothers for treating me badly. I recognized their feelings of resentment and strove to find ways to mitigate their sentiments. You can't know how someone will interpret your actions. People don't make bad decisions. The decisions they make seem good when they make them. They just go bad later. The consequences of seventeen years of resentment were profound as you will see.

Jacob openly rebuked me. I was unaccustomed to hearing criticism from my father. So, it came as quite a surprise to me that he interpreted my dream so negatively. I told him the dream because I didn't understand what it meant. He didn't give me the chance for further discussion, but I could tell he wondered if there was a deeper meaning involved. Twenty-two years would pass before all of us would grasp the significance of the dream.

Jacob put me in a leadership position. It was my job to go into the fields and assess how the work was progressing. On one occasion, I observed several breaches in the work environment. I reported them to Jacob. Naturally, the boys reacted negatively to my report, but I had been assigned a task and wanted to be true to what I was asked to do. It left a festering wound in the hearts of my older brothers. A wound that was just about ready to erupt. All that was needed was a flashpoint to ignite the vitriol.

Jacob had sent the boys to Shechem to tend to the flocks. He called for me to come to him. Once there, he assigned me the task of going to Shechem to see how things were going. When I arrived at Shechem, I could not find my brothers. As I searched for them, a man came up to me asking if he could be of any help. I told him no but inquired of him as to whether he had seen my brothers. He told me they left Shechem and travelled to Dothan. Dothan was situated on the trade route to Egypt. I hastily made my way in that direction.

Dothan was about a day's walk from Shechem. Since I was in a hurry, it didn't take me as long as it normally would to arrive at my destination. The boys were all gathered together talking. When they looked up and saw me coming from afar, they plotted to kill me. Each brother added some revenge into the conversation, raising the state of agitation to higher levels. One wanted to kill me first, and then throw me into one of the cisterns in the area. Another suggested just throwing me in the cistern. Still another wanted to kill me and tell Jacob that a wild animal had attacked me.

Reuben, the oldest sibling, talked the rest of the boys into putting me in a dried- up cistern to die. He told them this to keep them from killing me. His plan was to extract me from the well to save my life, so he planned later to come back and get me out of the pit.

As I entered the circle of brothers, they grabbed me and shoved me into a dry cistern deep enough that I could not get out. Even if I could climb out, they were right there to push me back down. I called out to them, begging for help, but my pleas only satisfied them more.

Reuben left the group for some unknown reason. Judah spoke up in his absence, saying, "Let's not kill him. He is still our brother." The boys listened to Judah and decided a better way of getting rid of me was to sell me into slavery. There was a trade route that went right past the location of the camp in which the boys were staying. A group of Ishmaelite traders came riding their camels. My brothers extracted me from the pit and sold me to them.

Despite my protestations, the Ishmaelites carried me away into captivity. In the meantime, Reuben returned to camp. He went to the pit to help me out of the oval prison in which I had been held. He called out to me, "Joseph, I have come to rescue you." There was no response. He called again. Still nothing. Finally, he went to the camp and learned that the boys sold me to the Ishmaelites. He screamed at the boys, "What have you done. Do you realize that I'll get the blame for this?" They concocted a story about a wild animal attacking me and all they could salvage was the multi-colored garment I was wearing. They took the garment doused it in animal blood and took it back to Jacob telling the story of how Joseph was killed by a wild animal.

Jacob was devastated. He vowed he would go to his grave in mourning. He was one hundred and eight years old when I was taken from him.

The Ishmaelites took me to Egypt where they sold me to Potiphar, the captain of Pharaoh's guard. The Lord was with me and prospered my way. Potiphar recognized how God had blessed me. Everything I did was successful. For that reason, he placed me in charge of everything he had. Potiphar's wife found me to be handsome and approached me to engage in a sexual relationship. I refused her advances. She interpreted my actions as playing hard to get, which made her all the more determined to have her way. She was accustomed to getting what she wanted.

I explained to her how Potiphar had faith in me and trusted me with everything he had. How could I betray that confidence and sin against Potiphar and God? This went on day after day.

Finally, exhausted with the failure to lure me into her bed, she grabbed my garments and would not let go. I pulled away from her with such force that my garments ripped at the seams and came off my body, leaving me naked in her presence. I ran from the house.

Potiphar's wife was so humiliated about being rejected that she concocted this story about me trying to rape her. The evidence was in her favor. She complained that Potiphar had brought this Hebrew into her house to laugh at her and attempt to have his way with her. Regardless of the truth of her statements, Potiphar had me cast into prison. This is the second time my freedom had been taken from me through no fault of my own.

It would have been easy for me to become despondent, but the Lord was with me and gave me hope amidst despair. He showered His unending love and favor upon me, causing me to have a positive attitude. The jailkeeper could not help but take notice of my attitude. He put me in charge of all the prisoners.

The baker and cupbearer of Pharaoh displeased him. They were confined in the same prison as me. The jailkeeper placed them in my charge. When they had been in custody for some time, they both came to me and shared a dream they had. The cupbearer shared his dream with me first. I listened intently and told the cupbearer that in three days Pharaoh would release him from prison and restore him to his former position. The cupbearer was appreciative of my interpretation of his dream. I asked him to remember me when he was in Pharaoh's company that I might be released as well.

The baker recounted his dream to me. For him I did not have good news. I told him that in three days Pharaoh would have him executed. Just as I had told them, three days passed by. On the third day Pharaoh called the two men together. He restored the cupbearer to his original status, but he had the baker executed. The cupbearer was so happy to be out of prison that he neglected to mention me to Pharaoh.

Two years went by. I was twenty-eight years old and had spent the past eleven years in captivity, part of which was in jail. Pharaoh had two dreams the same night. In his first dream there were seven healthy cows standing by the river Nile. Seven other cows looking thin and sickly came up out of the Nile and ate the seven healthy cows.

In the second dream, there were seven healthy ears of corn growing on one stalk. Another stalk sprouted up with seven ears of blighted corn. The blighted corn swallowed up the healthy corn. Pharaoh was upset by his dreams and called for the court magicians and wise men to interpret the dream. Unfortunately, they were unable to give an adequate explanation. The cupbearer remembered me and spoke to Pharaoh. When Pharaoh called for me I told him the seven healthy cows and the seven healthy stalks of corn represented seven years of plenty that would come over the land. But the years of plenty would be followed by seven years of famine, represented by the sickly-looking cows and the blighted corn.

I recommended that Pharaoh appoint someone to oversee gathering enough grain from the years of plenty to supplement the need for grain in the seven years of famine.

Pharaoh was impressed with my interpretation and named me as the prime minister of Egypt to carry out the plan I had outlined to him. I was thirty years old when I became the Prime Minister of Egypt. Pharaoh clothed me with royal garments and gave me a wife.

I implemented the plan by travelling around the country placing in reserve as much grain as possible to be available for the seven years of famine. The silos of Egypt were full.

During the seven years of plenty, I fathered two sons. The firstborn was Manasseh. His name means "forgetful" for God has caused me to forget all the hardships I had endured to this point. The second son is Ephraim. His name means "fruitful" for God has caused me to be fruitful in the land of my suffering.

Just as I had said, the seven years of plenty came to an end and the seven years of famine had begun. I was fully aware of the fact that the plan for the preservation of grain for the lean years was given to me by God. It was not my idea. Nonetheless, there was plenty of grain available in Egypt.

The famine extended beyond Egypt. Back in Canaan, Jacob was beginning to become concerned about grain for food. He called his sons together and instructed them to go to Egypt to buy grain, because he had heard grain was available there. Ten of his sons made the trip to buy grain. Benjamin, the youngest of the boys, remained behind with Jacob.

I was the person who decided if grain could be sold, and to whom it was sold. You can imagine my surprise when my ten brothers stood before me requesting to buy grain. I recognized them right away, but they did not recognize me. I quizzed them harshly, "Where are you from?"

They replied, "From Canaan."

"You are spies, trying to learn how much grain we have," I responded.

They answered, "No sir! We are twelve brothers, the sons of one man. Our youngest brother is not with us. He remained with our father in Canaan and one brother is no longer with us."

"No! You are spies. I will test you to prove to me who you are. You shall not be allowed to go until your younger brother is brought here. Send one of you to get your youngest brother and bring him here. The rest of you will remain in custody until the youngest brother arrives." I kept them in custody for three days.

On the third day of their incarceration, I said to them, "If you want to live, one of you will stay here and the others will go to get your youngest brother. I will send some grain with you. If you do this, you will verify your story. If not, you shall die."

The boys said to one another. "We are being paid back for what we did to Joseph. He begged us, and we did not listen"

Reuben spoke up, "I told you, but you would not listen. Now we are reaping what we sowed."

They were unaware that I had understood everything they said. I walked away from them and wept. Once I composed himself, I returned to them and asked which one was going to stay. Simeon was taken and bound before their very eyes. I gave orders to fill bags with grain for each brother and to place the money they had paid for the grain in their bag. The boys departed for Canaan.

As they were travelling, one of the boys opened his bag and discovered the money he had paid for the grain. He told his brothers. They didn't know what to think. Fear entered their hearts.

When they arrived in Canaan they told Jacob what had happened. They explained that Simeon was being held in prison until they returned with Benjamin. Jacob made it clear that there was no way he would send Benjamin. It made matters worse when all the boys opened their sacks to find the money they had paid for the grain.

Even though Simeon was in prison, Jacob would not relent. The famine took a toll on the family. The grain they had brought back from Egypt was almost gone. Jacob called the boys together and told them to go back to Egypt for more grain. The boys told him that the man in Egypt was very clear that he would not even see them if the youngest brother was not with them. Jacob got defensive. "Why did you tell him you had another brother?"

They replied, "He asked us questions about our family. He wanted to know if you were still alive. What were we supposed to do?"

Judah spoke up. "Send Benjamin with me. I will take the responsibility of bringing him back to you. If anything happens, the blame will be mine forever." If we had done this earlier, the whole ordeal would have been over."

Jacob relented and allowed Benjamin to go. He instructed the boys to take fruit, almonds, honey, and myrrh as gifts to the man. He also told them to take the money for the first batch of grain and return it along with the money to buy additional grain. He bade them farewell.

The boys did as Jacob said and began their journey back to Egypt. They arrived early in the morning and requested to see the prime minister. I came out to see them. When I saw Benjamin with them I instructed the steward to prepare a meal to be ready by noon. The meal was prepared, and the boys were taken to my house. They didn't know what to expect. They thought they would be imprisoned because of the money they found in their sacks. They spoke to the steward and told him about the money and how they wanted to repay it along with purchasing more grain. There was water to wash their feet, food for their animals, and a meal prepared for them.

They prepared to meet me and give me the gifts they brought with them. When I arrived, I asked them if their father was still alive and if so, how was he doing. They assured me that he was okay. I looked at Benjamin and asked if this was the youngest brother they spoke about the last time they were here.

The scene was more than my heart could take. I hastily made my way out of the room and wept. Once again, I regained my composure, washed my face, and rejoined the boys for the meal.

The seating arrangements for the meal were specific. I sat by myself with my staff at a separate table. The boys were seated at a third table and arranged according to birth order. As they were seated they looked at each other in dismay. Each brother received servings from my table with Benjamin receiving five times more than his brothers.

After the meal, I instructed my staff to fill the boy's sacks with as much food as they could carry, and to put the money they had paid for the food in the sack as well. They were also instructed to take my silver cup and put it in the sack of the youngest brother along with his money. At the next dawn, the boys were sent on their way back to Canaan.

They were gone only a short time when I instructed my stewards to go after them. When they reached them the steward was to say to them, "Why have you repaid evil for good? My master drinks from his cup and you have done evil by taking it."

The steward did as I instructed. They answered, "What are you talking about? We did not take the cup. We even brought back the money from the last time we were here."

The steward responded, "We will search your sacks. If we find the cup, we will take the guilty party into custody and let the rest of you go."

Beginning with the oldest, they searched each brother's sack. They found the cup in Benjamin's sack. All the brothers repacked their sacks and returned to the city with Benjamin.

Once in the city they were escorted to my house, where I was waiting for them. I demanded, "What have you done?"

Judah answered, "What can we do to make this right? God has revealed our transgression. We are all guilty."

I replied, "No! Only the one who had my cup in his sack will be my servant. The rest of you return to your father."

Judah approached me and said, "Please hear me out and don't be angry with us. The last time we were here you asked us if we had a father or a brother. We answered you honestly. We brought our youngest brother back at your request. We had a brother who is dead. We told you that if anything happens to this our youngest brother, that his father would not recover from the grief. I was able to bring him to you because I took full responsibility for his life. Please keep me as your captive and let the others go."

I could contain myself no longer. I had the servants clear the room except for my brothers. I wept so loud that it was easily heard outside the room. I turned to my brothers and said, "I am Joseph! Is my father still alive?"

My brothers were in shock and could not speak. I said to them, "I am Joseph whom you sold into slavery. Do not be distraught, God sent me here to preserve life. The famine has been with us for two years but there are five years of famine left to go. It was God Who sent me here not you. Hurry and go tell my father that I am alive. Bring him here to live in the land of Goshen. You will be near me and I will provide for you. Go tell my father all you have witnessed here concerning my position and the honor with which I have been entrusted."

After I spoke those words I hugged Benjamin and wept the more. I greeted each brother with a kiss and bade them hurry back.

Pharaoh heard about the meeting and supported me fully. We gave the boys wagons, clothing, and provisions for the journey to Canaan and the return trip. Benjamin received money plus five changes of clothing. To Jacob we sent animals loaded with food. We sent them on their way with the admonition not to fight, and hurry back with Jacob.

When they arrived in Canaan, Jacob was anxiously waiting to see Benjamin unharmed. When the boys told him that Joseph was alive, his heart almost stopped beating. They told him about Joseph's position in Egypt and the things he said to them. Jacob was ecstatic and prepared to leave for Egypt as soon as possible.

Jacob and the boys, along with their wives and children gathered together all their belongings and left for Beersheba, where Jacob offered a sacrifice to God. God spoke to him saying, "Do not be afraid to go to Egypt. There you will become a great nation. I will bring you back to this land. From Beersheba Jacob and all his descendants journeyed to Egypt with a total of sixty-six people.

When they drew close to Goshen, Jacob sent Judah on ahead to let me know the entourage was close. I went to Goshen to welcome them to Egypt. When they arrived, I rushed to Jacob, put my arms around him, and wept for joy. Jacob said, "Now, I can die in peace. I have seen your face and know that you are still alive.

I went to Pharaoh informing him that my father and brothers had made it back from Canaan. He was happy to meet them and instructed me to let them settle in the best part of Goshen. Jacob blessed Pharaoh. Pharaoh asked Jacob how old he was. Jacob told him one hundred thirty years.

Jacob lived in Egypt seventeen years and died at one hundred forty-seven years of age. Before he died, he spoke to each of his twelve sons. To some he criticized. To some he praised. To some he prophesied. But to Joseph he exacted a promise to bury him in Canaan.

Shortly thereafter the boys were summoned to Jacob's bedside. He commanded them to bury him with his fathers in the cave at Machpelah. Abraham and Isaac are buried there. When he finished speaking to them, he breathed his last.

I commanded the physicians to embalm Jacob and prepare for his burial in Canaan. Pharaoh granted me permission to travel to Canaan for the burial. After an appropriate time of grieving, we left for Canaan with Pharaoh's blessing. We buried Jacob just as he requested and returned to Goshen.

My brothers feared that since Jacob was no longer alive I might take a different attitude toward them. They told me that before he died Jacob told them to ask for my forgiveness. I told them they need not fear, "You meant evil against me, but God meant it for good."

I spoke these words to them. "Let it be known to your descendants that God will bring you out of this land and return you to the land He swore on oath to give to Abraham, Isaac, and Jacob. When that happens, my bones are to be carried to Canaan as well."

Before I died, I appointed my son Manasseh to be the family scribe.

PS: I Manasseh accept the role of family scribe and certify that Joseph, my father, lived to the age of one hundred ten years.

Here is the complete chart from Adam to Joseph.

Name	Year Born	Year Died	Age at Death
Adam	1	930	930
Seth	130	1042	912
Enosh	235	1050	815
Cainan	325	1235	910
Mahalel	395	1290	895
Jared	460	1422	962
Enoch	622		
Methuselah	687	1656	969
Lamech	874	1651	777
Noah	1056	2007	950
Shem	1558	2058	500
Flood	1656		
Arpachshad	1658	2096	438
Salah	1693	2126	433
Eber	1723	2188	464
Peleg	1757	1996	239
Reu	1787	2026	239
Serug	1819	2049	230
Nahor	1849	1997	148
Terah	1878	2083	205
Abram	2009	2184	175
Isaac	2109	2289	180
Jacob	2169	2316	147
Joseph	2260	2370	110

May they all rest in peace.

www.ingramcontent.com/pod-product-compliance
Lightning Source LLC
Chambersburg PA
CBHW022009120526
44592CB00034B/751